Good uestions for Math Teaching

Why Ask Them and What to Ask, Grades 5–8

Lainie Schuster
Nancy Canavan Anderson

Math Solutions
Sausalito, California, USA

Math Solutions
150 Gate 5 Road
Sausalito, CA 94965
www.mathsolutions.com

Library of Congress Cataloging-in-Publication Data
Schuster, Lainie.
    Good questions for math teaching : why ask them and
what to ask, grades 5–8 / Lainie Schuster, Nancy Canavan Anderson.
        p. cm.
    Includes bibliographical references.
    ISBN 0-941355-69-1 (acid-free paper)
    1. Mathematics—Study and teaching (Elementary).
2. Questioning.   I. Anderson, Nancy Canavan.   II. Title.
QA 135.6.S435 2005
372.7—dc22   2005010703

ISBN-13: 978-0-941355-69-8

Editor: Toby Gordon
Production: Melissa L. Inglis
Cover design: Catherine Hawkes/Cat and Mouse
Interior design: Joni Doherty Design
Composition: Interactive Composition Corporation

SUSTAINABLE FORESTRY INITIATIVE
Label applies to the text stock
Certified Fiber Sourcing
www.sfiprogram.org

Printed in the United States of America on acid-free paper
14   13   12   11   ML   9   10

A Message from Math Solutions

We at Math Solutions believe that teaching math well calls for increasing our understanding of the math we teach, seeking deeper insights into how students learn mathematics, and refining our lessons to best promote students' learning.

Math Solutions shares classroom-tested lessons and teaching expertise from our faculty of professional development consultants as well as from other respected math educators. Our publications are part of the nationwide effort we've made since 1984 that now includes

- more than five hundred face-to-face professional development programs each year for teachers and administrators in districts across the country;
- professional development books that span all math topics taught in kindergarten through high school;
- videos for teachers and for parents that show math lessons taught in actual classrooms;
- on-site visits to schools to help refine teaching strategies and assess student learning; and
- free online support, including grade-level lessons, book reviews, inservice information, and district feedback, all in our Math Solutions Online Newsletter.

For information about all of the products and services we have available, please visit our website at *www.mathsolutions.com.* You can also contact us to discuss math professional development needs by calling (800) 868-9092 or by sending an email to *info@mathsolutions.com.*

We're always eager for your feedback and interested in learning about your particular needs. We look forward to hearing from you.

Contents

Acknowledgments

Peter Sullivan and Pat Lilburn's *Good Questions for Math Teaching: Why Ask Them and What to Ask, K–6* (2002) has been the model for much of our work in this book. Sullivan and Lilburn's book has been extremely popular with teachers because of its content, format, and user-friendliness. We hope our book will complement theirs.

We teach in an era of wonderful resources and standards-based curricula. Our teaching has continued to develop and improve because of them. We would like to acknowledge the following series, publications, and their authors, from which we adapted many of our questions: *Everyday Mathematics* (Everyday Learning Corporation 2002); *Math Matters* (Chapin and Johnson 2000); the Connected Mathematics Project series (Prentice Hall 2002); the Hot Topics in Math series (Dale Seymour Publications 2001), and the Investigations in Number, Data, and Space series (Scott Foresman 2004).

We both have been extremely fortunate to have had opportunities to work with Dr. Suzanne Chapin. Her influence on our professional lives has been enormous. Suzanne is a colleague, a teacher, a mentor, and a wonderful friend.

We cannot think of any one person who has more influenced the teaching of mathematics than Marilyn Burns. Marilyn's vision and passion for thinking mathematically are what push us to ask the "good" questions.

We would also like to give special thanks to our reader, Joan Carlson, and our editor, Toby Gordon. Joan's suggestions and edits kept us grounded and focused. Toby's questions kept reminding us of what was important. We became better writers and better mathematical thinkers because of them both.

It is our students, however, who continue to inspire, motivate, and surprise us. This book is written for them.

LAINIE SCHUSTER
NANCY CANAVAN ANDERSON

PART ONE

The Practice of Good Questioning

Questions may be one of the most powerful technologies invented by humans. Even though they require no batteries and need not be plugged into the wall, they are tools which help us make up our minds, solve problems, and make decisions.

—Jamie McKenzie

"Good" questions can set the stage for meaningful classroom discussion and learning. When we ask good questions in math class, we invite our students to think, to understand, and to share a mathematical journey with their classmates and teachers alike. Students are no longer passive receivers of information when asked questions that challenge their understandings and convictions about mathematics. They become active and engaged in the construction of their own mathematical understanding and knowledge.

As we work to emphasize problem solving, application of concepts and procedures, and the development of a variety of thinking skills in our mathematics curricula, it becomes vital that we pay increased attention to the improvement of our questioning techniques in mathematics lessons, according to Peter Sullivan and Pat Lilburn, authors of *Good Questions for Math Teaching: Why Ask Them and What to Ask, K–6* (2002) and upon whose work this book is modeled. As teachers of mathematics, we want our students not only to understand *what* they think but also to be able to articulate *how* they arrived at those understandings. Developing productive questions can help focus learning on the process of thinking while attending to the study of content (Dantonio and Beisenherz 2001, 60). Good questions created and posed by teachers ultimately become powerful tools for student learning.

1 What Are Good Questions?

Careful, intentional, and mindful questioning is one of the most powerful tools a skillful teacher possesses (Costa and Kallick 2000, 34). So what do good questions "look" like?

- They help students *make sense* of the mathematics.
- They are *open-ended,* whether in answer or approach. There may be multiple answers or multiple approaches.
- They empower students to *unravel their misconceptions.*
- They not only *require the application of facts and procedures* but encourage students to *make connections and generalizations.*
- They are *accessible to all student*s in their language and offer an entry point for all students.
- Their answers *lead students to wonder more about a topic* and to perhaps construct new questions themselves as they investigate this newly found interest.

2 How Are Good Questions Created?

While teacher guides provide direction and offer questions to ask, it is the teacher who must craft good questions to guide students to new learning and understanding.

Creating good questions relies heavily on the destination we have in mind. What do we expect our students to be able to do, say, or understand by the end of the lesson? Beginning with the end in mind requires us to start with a clear understanding of desired knowledge, learning, and outcomes. When we think about questions that we might ask our students, it is helpful to consider these issues:

- the mathematical goals of the lesson
- the misconceptions students may have
- the connections we'd like students to make between lesson goals and previously covered concepts and/or procedures
- assessment of understanding

The questions in this book may help you begin a unit of study. They may help students make connections between new material and previously covered concepts and procedures. They may offer opportunities for students to confront faulty thinking or fragile understanding. There are also those questions that encourage students to wonder and that push *them* to pose new questions as they seek greater understanding.

3 What Are the Teacher's Responsibilities in Presenting Good Questions?

When presenting good questions, it is essential for teachers to

- ▓ understand the mathematics embedded in the question
- ▓ present the question clearly using accessible mathematical language
- ▓ set clear and reasonable expectations for student work
- ▓ allow for individual approaches, methods, and/or answers
- ▓ add variety or more data to a question to ensure accessibility for all students
- ▓ make good use of concrete materials
- ▓ allow ample time for discovery and consolidation of answers, strategies, and the discovered mathematics

Someone somewhere said, "It's all in the presentation," and correct he or she was. In order to engage students and make the process of answering a question meaningful, we need to be mindful of our presentation and expectations. It is important for teachers to work through a question before presenting it to students—to solve it and think through it themselves. This is of particular importance with open questions since these questions have many different approaches and/or answers. Try to think of more than just one response. Doing so will help you anticipate and then react to the variety of responses you will hear from your students. Undoubtedly, students will think of things you did not! In addition to working through the question, think about the following:

- ▓ Do I have the necessary materials (for example, graph paper, chart paper, manipulatives)? If not, where can I get them?
- ▓ What misconceptions or difficulties might my students have with the language, concepts, or directions?

- What follow-up questions can I ask that will readdress or redirect misconceptions or difficulties?
- How much time will students need to answer the question?

Working through good mathematics takes time. An understanding of the mathematics involved in the question being presented will help you determine the amount of time a question may take to answer and process. It is important, however, that you give ample time to discussing both students' answers and the reasoning behind those answers. Students need enough time to fully develop a thought or conjecture as answers are discussed. Because we are so pressed for time in our classrooms, we often give more time to question *answering* than to *processing*. Having students share and discuss answers and strategies can be as important to learning as the act of answering. There may be those times when a question and its answers take on a life of their own—and a full math period! Please allow that to happen once in a while. Students will take greater ownership of their thinking and learning when they realize that it is *they* who are determining the course of study.

4 What Classroom Conditions Are Necessary to Support Good Answers?

To question well is to teach well. Good questioning practice requires classroom routines that may take time and patience to establish but will be well worth the time and effort. It should also be noted that not only can we enrich our mathematics instruction by employing these practices, but adapting similar routines in other disciplines may improve student understanding and engagement in those areas as well.

Creating a Safe Environment

The teaching and learning of mathematics can be an emotionally charged practice. Teachers and students come to the table with different sets of expectations and proficiencies. When good questions are presented in a safe classroom environment, learning, communication, and enthusiasm can quickly ensue. Students are taking risks when they answer open-ended questions. Because there is often not just one correct answer or process, students need to be encouraged to keep open minds and support the thinking of their peers. Disagreements will occur . . . and we hope they do! Some of our most powerful learning occurs as we try to prove or disprove what appears to be faulty thinking. Students need to realize, however, that they may disagree with another's *ideas,* which is quite different from disagreeing with the person himself. Students are to treat each other civilly and with respect. This may take vigilant monitoring on the part of the teacher as a mathematically safe environment is developed and maintained.

A Place to Begin

Considering how students may begin the process of answering a question can be an important issue in many classrooms. You may need to make adjustments in the language and/or directions of the posed question in order to support struggling students and even those students who always seem to get it quickly.

Waiting

Purposeful, consistent, and patient wait time will ultimately increase engagement and active participation. If our goal is to elicit mindful, insightful, and mathematically sound answers, then we need to give our students time to think and formulate their conjectures and answers before opening up classroom discussions. We live in a world of immediacy, so asking students to use the silence of wait time to think and formulate their answers before starting a conversation can be difficult for everyone involved. Employing the five-second rule after each time you ask a question or call on a student will help establish this important practice.

Discussing Answers

Once students have had enough time to formulate an answer to a question, they benefit from hearing one another's answers. First, ask students to talk in a small-group format—either in pairs or with table groups. Multiple conversations can occur, and the teacher should circulate and take notice of generated insights, strategies, partial understandings, and misconceptions. These small-group conversations often give students the time and opportunity to rehearse their thinking. Students may be more willing to share their reasoning and ideas with the whole class once they have first had a chance to practice with a small group. Students need to be encouraged and reminded to keep written records of their thinking together—calculations, charts, diagrams, and/or pictures. This documentation will help them support and defend their thinking and answers.

When it is time for the talk to move to a whole-class discussion, the teacher can guide the conversation by keeping the focus on the students' thinking. Students need to be encouraged to support, add to, and even disagree with the strategies, insights, and answers of fellow classmates. They also need to address one another, not merely the teacher. This may be a new approach for both

Good Questions for Math Teaching

teachers and students. Class discussions offer opportunities for students to achieve understanding by processing information, applying reasoning, hearing ideas from others, and connecting new thinking to what they already know (Chapin, O'Connor, and Anderson 2003). The following list offers a generic set of questions that may help guide and facilitate discussions of students' answers:

- Why do you think that?
- How did you know to try that strategy?
- How do you know you have an answer?
- Will this work with every number? Every similar situation?
- When will this strategy not work? Can you give a counterexample?
- Who has a different strategy?
- How is your answer like or different from another student's?
- Can you repeat your classmate's ideas in your own words?
- Do you agree or disagree with your classmate's idea? Why?

PART TWO

How to Use This Book

The questions in this book are designed as a supplement to your mathematics curriculum. As you progress through a unit of study, you may want to ask your students questions in this book that correspond to that unit. Embedding questions from this book within your lessons may further enhance student learning and understanding. When studying angles, for example, you may wish to refer to questions in this book to support, extend, or enrich your present curriculum. If current practice has your students identifying specific pairs of angles as vertical, adjacent, or linear, you may wish to ask students what a Venn diagram might look like if they were to sort these angles as posed by Question 2 on page 85. By constructing an answer to this question, students will deepen their understanding of these angles by generalizing the relationships among them.

Another way to use this book is to use the questions as a daily warm-up activity. This is a particularly effective approach in the middle grades, when students often switch classes and enter the classroom in a five-minute time span. Before the students enter the room, write the question on the board. You may choose a question that corresponds to the current unit or a question that requires students to review a particularly challenging or important skill or concept. Once the students enter and get settled, they can write their answers in their mathematics notebooks or journals. You can then begin the class with a discussion of students' answers. This routine makes good use of transition time while immediately focusing math class on reasoning and communication.

In addition to using these questions during instructional time, you could assign them for homework or incorporate them in your assessments. Typically, math homework and assessment practices tend to focus on skills and/or closed questions that require recall of what was learned in class. If your students usually complete a review worksheet of the day's lesson, attach (or even substitute) a question from this book that will require them to think beyond what they have learned, to connect an understanding from a previous lesson, or to confront a misconception that may have arisen during class. In addition, if students' assessments normally include computations and problems for which there is only one correct answer, adapt those assessments to include some questions from this book that will allow students to think creatively about the mathematics they are learning.

The power of questioning is in the answering. As teachers, we not only need to ask good questions to get good answers but need to ask good questions to promote the thinking required to give good answers.

Perhaps the Dodecahedron, Norton Juster's renowned mathematician in *The Phantom Tollbooth,* says it all best:

> "That's absurd," objected Milo, whose head was spinning from all the numbers and questions.
>
> "That may be true," the Dodecahedron acknowledged, "but if it's completely accurate, and as long as the answer is right, who cares if the question is wrong? If you want sense, you'll have to make it yourself." (1961, 175)

PART THREE

Good Questions to Use in Math Class

The questions in this book are divided into seven strands:

> number relationships
> multiplication and proportional reasoning
> fractions, decimals, and percents
> geometry
> algebraic thinking
> data analysis and probability
> measurement

Each strand is subdivided into two bilevel grade spans: 5–6 and 7–8.

A set of learning objectives and necessary materials are listed at the beginning of each section to help guide your content and question choices. Many of the presented questions can be adapted to meet the needs of a particular class.

You may wish to explore questions in both grade spans as you decide upon appropriate questions for your particular class. For example, if you teach sixth grade and your students have a thorough understanding of multiplication and proportional reasoning, you may want to explore questions from the 7–8 grade span. Similarly, if you teach seventh grade and find that your particular curriculum is more closely aligned with the grades 5–6 learning objectives of a particular strand, incorporate questions from that span within your teaching.

In general, the questions in each section are neither hierarchical nor sequential. Each can be posed individually. Each section can be viewed as an à la carte menu of question choices to help students deepen their understanding of the mathematics they are studying.

Following most questions are teacher notes. Some identify important teaching points while others describe in more depth the mathematics being addressed or misconceptions that may present themselves. Teaching notes may also present possible extensions or questions that can be assigned as homework, as noted by the **H** icon. As you pose questions in your classes, you may also wish to add your own teaching notes that you can use to guide instruction in subsequent years.

5 Number Relationships

When we ask students questions about relationships, properties, and procedures associated with number concepts, we help our students make important mathematical connections between numbers and their representations.

Grades 5–6

EXPERIENCES AT THIS LEVEL WILL HELP CHILDREN TO
- link dimensions of array models with factors and products
- identify relationships among factors, multiples, divisors, and products
- develop strategies to solve problems involving factors and multiples
- identify characteristics of various number classifications such as even, odd, prime, composite, square, and triangular

MATERIALS
- color tiles
- graph paper (see Blackline Masters)
- rules for *Fair Game 2* (see Blackline Masters)
- dot paper (see Blackline Masters)

Good Questions and Teacher Notes: Factors and Multiples

The vocabulary of number theory is relatively new to fifth and sixth graders. We need to listen very carefully to the mathematical talk of our students to support their correct use of the terminology. Although many fifth and sixth graders instinctively understand the terms *factor* and *multiple,* it becomes increasingly necessary to offer a variety of experiences in which children can use and apply newly defined mathematical words and classifications.

1. How many different arrays can you make with twelve tiles? Construct them. Reproduce each array on graph paper [see Blackline Masters] and label the dimensions of each array.

> Include the turnaround facts (e.g., 3×4 and 4×3). They are actually different arrays because of their different orientations.

How many arrays have you constructed? What are the *factor pairs* of twelve? How many factors are there of twelve? What do you notice about the number of arrays, the number of factor pairs, and the number of factors of twelve? Will this finding apply to any other numbers and their arrays, factors, and factor pairs?

> Pushing children to see the connection between the number of factor pairs, the number of arrays, and the number of factors of a specific number can be powerful. Factoring becomes purposeful. Understanding becomes grounded in visual experience. Children can use these visual models to support their ideas and conjectures about numbers and their properties.

2. Study the arrays of these numbers: twelve, twenty-four, thirty-six, and forty-eight. What are the properties that could help you classify these numbers into one group? If you added another number to this group, what could it be?

> Possible student answers could be:
>
> They are all divisible by two. (How do you know?)
>
> They are all divisible by twelve. (Can you show me?)
>
> They are all divisible by two and three. (Can we make a conjecture about the divisibility rules of six?)
>
> They are all divisible by two and four. (Are all numbers divisible by two also divisible by four? Is the reverse true? That is, are all numbers divisible by four also divisible by two?)
>
> Carefully crafted questions that probe the depth of children's understanding, which may be initially fragile, can make for rich classroom discussion. If children are encouraged to support their positions and give mathematical proof as they talk, their understanding will deepen.

3. Here is a set of numbers: {2, 3, 5, 7, 11, 13, 17}. What do these numbers have in common? How are they alike?

Good Questions for Math Teaching

They each have two factor pairs, two arrays, and two factors. They are prime.

Visual representations of numbers and concepts continue to be important for students of this age. This activity gives students the opportunity to create a visual representation for a prime number.

4. What do you notice about the array for one? How is it different from other numbers and their arrays? Support your conjecture with what you already know about prime and composite numbers.

There is a single array, and it is only 1 by 1. It is neither prime nor composite because it does not fit the classification generalization for either prime or composite numbers.

5. What other classifications can you use to group numbers? Use arrays and writing to support your groupings. Create sets of numbers and ask others to identify your grouping rule or principle.

Children may group numbers by divisibility, multiples, exponential progressions (even if they do not realize that that is what they are doing!), odd/even, and so on.

6. What is the smallest number that has three and four as factors?

Questions 6, 7, and 8 all have to do with common multiples, but they use factors to identify the product. This can be difficult for some children. It can even be difficult for some adults! If three and four have no common factors between them other than one, then the smallest multiple common to both is their product.

7. What is the smallest number that has four and six as factors?

Four and six share common factors, so we can assume the common multiple is less than the product of this pair of numbers. Rather than presenting children with a recipe, pose even more questions that will allow them to begin to formulate their own generalizations:

 Find pairs of numbers for which the common multiple is equal to the product of the pair. Find pairs of numbers for which the common multiple is less than the product of the pair. What do you notice about these two sets of pairs? Which pairs have common factors? Which do not?

8. For a given pair of numbers, how can you tell whether the least common multiple will be less than or equal to their product?

Questions 6 and 7 lead up to this particular question. Identifying common factors of a pair of numbers can help us determine how to find the least common multiple of that same pair of numbers. Writing about this generalization can reveal students' understandings as well as their misconceptions.

9. The weather is reported every 18 minutes on WFAC and every 12 minutes on WTOR. Both stations broadcast the weather at 1:30. When is the next time the stations will broadcast the weather at the same time?

> Common-multiple problems are much more engaging when a context is given. Having children make up their own common-multiple problems can prove to be extremely entertaining as well as mathematically revealing.

10. Will every multiplication problem create a rectangular array? If so, why does this occur?

> This question will help students think about the relationship between the equal-groupings notion of multiplication and the resulting equal rows and columns of a rectangular array.

11. How do you know when you have found all of the possible factors for a given number? What is the greatest factor possible for any whole number? Why does this make sense?

> These questions will help students develop efficient strategies for finding factors.

12. Do you think that it makes sense to split a day into twenty-four hours? Would another number have been a better choice? Why or why not?

> Linking mathematical questions to real-life problem solving helps students validate their learning.

Good Questions and Teacher Notes: Even and Odd

1. What makes twelve an even or odd number? Use an array to support your position.

> A discussion of divisibility can begin with this activity. The idea that an array of an even number can be equally divided into two parts can move children beyond the premise that an even number is a "double" and toward the idea that every even number is divisible by two.
>
> Do not allow children to dismiss questions pertaining to odd and even numbers as too simple. It becomes increasingly important, as well as interesting, to revisit big ideas to assess further understanding and increased conceptual application.

Good Questions for Math Teaching

2. Is the sum of two odd numbers odd or even? Is the sum of two even numbers odd or even? What about the sum of an odd and an even number? Justify your thinking using words, symbols, drawings, or tiles.

> Arrays can again be helpful as children work to articulate what constitutes evenness or oddness. The ability to evenly pair up counters in an array designates an even number whereas leftover counters designate an odd number. Children may also identify the odd-even sequence of counting numbers, which can also determine evenness or oddness.
>
> Introducing children to a matrix as an aid to charting outcomes is also of great help.

+	Even	Odd
Even	e	o
Odd	o	e

3. Is the product of two odd numbers odd or even? Is the product of two even numbers odd or even? What about the product of an odd and an even number? Justify your thinking using words, symbols, drawings, or tiles.

> Comparing the outcomes between the addition and multiplication of even and odd numbers can quickly lead to mathematically rich discussions. Issues of probability can generate more thought-provoking questions. For example, you could use this line of questioning with your students: If you were given a point each time you rolled an even sum with two dice and your partner received the same rolling an odd sum, who would have the better chance of winning? If you were given a point each time you rolled an even product with two dice and your partner received the same rolling an odd product, who would have a better chance of winning?
>
> A matrix is again helpful to chart outcomes.

×	Even	Odd
Even	e	e
Odd	e	o

4. Choose a partner and play a game of *Fair Game 2* [see Blackline Masters] [Burns 2000]. Using what you know about the sums and products of odd and even numbers, answer the following questions. Explain your reasoning for both

Number Relationships

the addition and the multiplication version. Is either game fair? Which player would you rather be? How could you make the game more fair?

> Charting the data from these games is important. Students can make conjectures as to the fairness of each game by analyzing their data. They may also realize that the matrices used in answering Questions 2 and 3 can also be helpful in supporting their "fair" or "not fair" positions.

Number Model	Player A Points	Player B Points
$5 + 1 = 6$	1	0
$6 + 1 = 7$	0	1
$6 + 1 = 7$	0	1
$3 + 4 = 7$	0	1

. . .

5. Is zero an even or an odd number?

> The odd-even-odd-even pattern of counting numbers or the odd-even-odd-even distribution of numbers on a number line is helpful in constructing a meaningful answer to this question. Too often, even older elementary-age children consider zero to be a nonnumber. Answering this question will cause some shift in thinking about the value of zero and what it "does" to and for numbers like twenty, two hundred, two thousand, and so on.

6. Make a case for why each number could *not* belong. Use words such as *factor, multiple, odd, even, prime,* and *composite* to support your position.

> 24, 12, 2, 11

> Asking students to identify more than one numeric relationship within a given set of numbers will help them develop the flexibility of reasoning often required by mathematical investigations.

7. I am thinking of four odd numbers.

> They are divisible by five.
> The sums of the digits of each number create a consecutive number sequence.
> My first number is a square number.
> What are my four numbers?

Good Questions for Math Teaching

Asking students to generate multiple sets of numbers that comply with an organizing principle can deepen understanding of those classifications. One answer is the numbers twenty-five, thirty-five, forty-five, and fifty-five.

Good Questions and Teacher Notes: Polygonal Numbers

1. Using dot paper, make a 1-by-1 array, a 2-by-2 array, and a 3-by-3 array [see Blackline Masters]. Outline the squares.

These are the first three "square" numbers. What would the next square number be? Justify your thinking. List or diagram the square numbers up to one hundred. Why are these numbers called square numbers?

> Children are fascinated by patterns, especially those that work for an entire classification of numbers.

2. What is the tenth square number? How do you know?

> Using the information from Question 1, we can determine that the sixth square number makes a 6-by-6 array, the seventh, a 7-by-7 array, and so on. The tenth square number would make a 10-by-10 array. Introducing the use of exponents as a symbolic representation is helpful and contextually relevant.

3. Can a square number be a prime number? Why or why not?

> Square numbers cannot be prime by definition. They have an odd number of factors (the least number of factors being three) and are the only classification of numbers that do.
>
> Asking students why this is so can help children uncover properties of square numbers.

4. Which square numbers are odd? Which are even? Can you describe a pattern demonstrated by consecutive square numbers? Will the seventeenth square number be odd or even? What about the eighteenth?

> Generalizing patterns is a fundamental prealgebraic skill. Connecting words to physical and symbolic representations is a skill too often ignored for children of this age.

5. I am thinking of a two-digit number. It is odd. It has exactly three factors. What number(s) might I be thinking of? Think of a final clue so that there is just one final solution.

> Once students begin to investigate different topics related to number theory, it becomes increasingly important to link those topics together so that students can begin to develop a web of understanding.
>
> Asking students to generate their own number riddles about square numbers (or any other type of number) can support their understanding as well.

6. These are the first three "triangular" numbers:

Diagram the next three triangular numbers on dot paper [see Blackline Masters]. What patterns do you see? Describe or diagram the tenth triangular number. What do you know about triangular numbers?

> It may be necessary for children to represent triangular numbers on dot paper before they can generate their properties and/or patterns in words.
>
> Children may want to pose their own questions about triangular numbers. Is there an odd-even sequence? Are any triangular numbers square numbers as well?

Grades 7–8

EXPERIENCES AT THIS LEVEL WILL HELP STUDENTS TO

- sort numbers into classes (prime, composite, polygonal, etc.)
- use the prime factors of a number to describe characteristics of the number
- relate integers to other classes of numbers
- find the absolute value of a number
- operate on integers
- read and write very large numbers using exponential, scientific, and calculator notation
- estimate the sizes of square roots

MATERIALS
■ calculators
■ rulers

Good Questions and Teacher Notes

1. Explain how each number below is different from all of the others.

81    $\sqrt{81}$ 36   14

> Make a list of students' reasons as they offer them. Look back at the vocabulary in their reasons, which may include the terms *divisor*, *factor*, and *divisible by*. Discuss the relationships between these terms. For example, suppose one student says, "The number fourteen is the only number that does not have nine as a factor," and another student says, "The number fourteen doesn't belong because it is the only number that is not divisible by nine." Use these two statements to discuss the relationship between the terms *factor* and *divisible by*.

2. The students in Mr. Mila's class want to know how old he is. Mr. Mila told them, "My age can be written as the sum of consecutive odd numbers starting from one." How old might Mr. Mila be?

> Once students notice that the possible ages are all square numbers, help them see this generalization by creating a set of nested squares beginning with one square, then adding three squares around it to create a 2-by-2 square, and so on.
>
> EXTENSION   As an extension to this question, you could ask the students to choose one age from the list of possibilities and write one final clue that would eliminate all but that number.

3. Carl and Angela are having a mathematical debate. Carl thinks you can determine only the prime factors of a number by examining its prime factorization. Angela thinks you can determine all of a number's factors by examining its prime factorization. Whose position do you support? Why?

> Students sometimes consider prime factorization as an exercise in math class without realizing that it is, in fact, a powerful tool for finding the factors of a number, especially large numbers.

4. Four students in Mrs. Burge's math class were comparing locker numbers. They made the following observations:

Our four locker numbers are relatively prime to one another.
Exactly two of our locker numbers are prime.

What might the students' locker numbers be?

> Post students' answers and verify as a class whether or not they meet the given criteria. Then discuss the distinction between the terms *prime* and *relatively prime*.

5. Yanira is working on a homework assignment from math class. She needs to find the opposites of integers such as $^+$12 and $^-$48. Yanira wonders, "Does every integer have an opposite? Since zero is an integer, does it have an opposite?" What do you think about Yanira's questions?

> Every integer will have an opposite since the number line extends infinitely in both directions. A common misconception is that zero has no opposite when it is actually its own opposite.

6. Mohini and Paul were placing numbers on a number line. Mohini said, "My number is greater than yours."
Paul agreed but added, "My number has a greater absolute value than yours." What could Paul and Mohini's numbers be?

> Since *absolute value* is defined as a number's distance from zero, encourage students to use a number line to answer this question. Paul's number must be negative but farther from zero than Mohini's is.

7. For homework, Kim Lee was adding integers. He looked at a computation and said, "I know the sign of the sum will be negative." Based on Kim Lee's statement, what do you know about the computation?

> This question aims to help students generalize about the relationship between the sign of the sum and the numbers in an integer addition problem. Students may need to make a list of integer addition problems whose sums are negative and look for commonalities among them in order to answer this question.

8. Annie added three integers and got a sum of zero. What might the integers have been? [Sullivan and Lilburn 2002]

One way to find three integers whose sum is zero is to think of a pair of opposites and write one as the sum of two integers. For example, $^-10 + 10 = {}^-10 + 4 + 6 = 0$.

9. Zach looked at an integer subtraction computation and said, "You can find the difference between these two integers by doubling the first integer." What might the computation have been?

> Make a list of students' answers and ask them what they notice. Each computation will be a pair of integer opposites. Once students discover this, link this idea to multiplying the first integer by two. For example, $^-7 - 7 = {}^-14$ can also be written as $^-7 \times 2 = {}^-14$.

10. Mannie multiplied three integers and got a product of $^-48$. What might the integers have been?

> Post students' answers to this question and ask them what generalizations they notice among them. Doing so will help students understand the relationships between the signs of factors and corresponding products.

11. Nan's Donut Shop has been in business for one month. Each week, Nan looks at her income and expenses to determine her profit (income − expenses = profit). Nan has determined that her average weekly profit is $^-\$40$. What might have been Nan's income and expenses *each* week?

> If students are unfamiliar with using money to learn about integers, you may need to discuss what $^-\$40$ means before asking students to answer this question.

12. Katya earns $5 a day in allowance and spends $3 a day on lunch and other necessities. What number sentence could Katya use to determine how much money she has after any number of days?

> Student-generated number sentences might include the following:

$$(5 \times n) - (3 \times n) = t$$
$$5n - (3n) = t$$
$$2n = t$$

> where $n =$ number of days; $t =$ total amount of money
> Ask students to identify what is the same and what is different among their answers. Comparing and contrasting number sentences will help students identify relationships among them.

Number Relationships

13. Niles kept track of the temperature outside his home from noon until midnight. Upon looking back at the data, he noticed that the rule $50 + (^-0.5)h = t$ (where h equals the number of hours after noon and t equals the temperature) could be used to find the temperature at any given time. How did the temperature change over the course of this day?

> Too often students can plug values into expressions that use variables without understanding the expressions. It is just as important to spend time discussing the meaning of expressions as it is to evaluate them.

14. The population of the United States is estimated to be 2.8×10^8. What might be the actual population?

> Exploring scientific notation using real-world data makes the topic relevant to middle grades students.

15. A popular new CD has earned $12.3 million in sales. What might be the actual sales?

> Discussing students' answers to this question offers an opportunity to review elementary place value concepts in the middle grades.

16. Rich used his calculator to estimate how many times his heart has beaten since birth. After he did a series of calculations to determine this number, "4.79E8" appeared on the calculator's screen. How might Rich have interpreted this number?

> Students need to learn how to use calculators, like any other tool, to solve problems. For example, students often need to figure out how to interpret the number that appears on the screen. While the output styles vary, calculators often use the notation shown above to express numbers that are too large to fit on the screen. Scientific notation can be used to interpret these numbers. For example, 4.79E8 means that the number is close to 4.79×10^8, or 479,000,000.

17. Randy needed to estimate the size of a square root. He looked at the square root and said, "Well, I know it is between ten and eleven." What do you think the square root was?

> Estimating the size of square roots is an important part of developing number sense in the middle grades.

18. Place one square root, one integer, and one fraction on the number line below. How did you decide where to place your numbers?

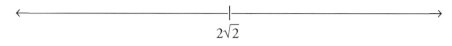

$2\sqrt{2}$

> This question can be modified by changing the requirements or the given square root.

19. Kaelen used the Pythagorean theorem to measure the hypotenuse of a right triangle. She reported that the hypotenuse was between 8 and 9 units. What might have been the measurements of the legs of the triangle?

> While this question may be better classified as a measurement question, it offers students a meaningful application of square roots. One way to answer this question is to think of 8 as $\sqrt{64}$ and 9 as $\sqrt{81}$. Then, find two numbers whose squares have a sum that is greater than $\sqrt{64}$ but less than $\sqrt{81}$.

20. In math class, Brianna used the Pythagorean theorem to find the measurement of the hypotenuse of a right triangle whose legs were two and three inches. Once she found the measurement, $\sqrt{13}$, her teacher said, "Use your ruler to check your answers." But Brianna said, "How can I use my ruler when it does not show square roots?" What do you think Brianna's teacher had in mind? How could Brianna have used a ruler to check her answers?

> Using a ruler to explore square roots will help students approximate the size of square roots using what they know about whole numbers and fractions.

21. Mateo used the steps below to find the perimeter of an isosceles right triangle whose side lengths measured $\sqrt{8}$, $\sqrt{8}$, and 4 units:

$$\sqrt{8} + \sqrt{8} = \sqrt{16} = 4$$
$$4 + 4 = 8$$
$$Perimeter = 8 \ units$$

What do you think of Mateo's method?

> Students often think that $\sqrt{a} + \sqrt{b} = \sqrt{a + b}$. This is a common misconception that can be disproved by estimating the size of the square roots being added. For example, $\sqrt{8}$ is greater than 2 since $\sqrt{4} = 2$. The sum of $\sqrt{8} + \sqrt{8}$ would, therefore, be greater than 4, not equal to 4.

6 Multiplication and Proportional Reasoning

The study of multiplication, division, and proportional reasoning can promote procedural competency and conceptual understanding. Asking questions that require students to understand and articulate multiplication and division can help develop these skills.

Grades 5–6

EXPERIENCES AT THIS LEVEL WILL HELP CHILDREN TO

- understand the language of multiplication and division situations
- refine methods of multiplication and division
- decompose factors to make sense of multiplicative properties and procedures
- interpret two types of division situations: partitive and quotative
- interpret remainders within the context of a story problem
- apply rules of divisibility
- set up and solve proportions

MATERIALS

- calculators
- colored pencils
- graph paper (see Blackline Masters)

Although procedural competency is an important goal in the teaching of multiplication and division, the questions in this section are designed to promote and establish further conceptual understanding and knowledge of these operations.

Good Questions and Teacher Notes

1. Create a story problem that involves multiplying the factors thirty-six and seventeen. Give a written explanation of how you could solve the problem.

> Written explanations of solutions can help identify understandings and misconceptions. Story problems written by students of this age should demonstrate multiplicative relationships rather than additive (repeated addition) ones.

2. $? \times ? = 612$

What might the missing numbers be? How many solutions can you find? Use one of the number models you found to create a story problem. Include the missing factors in your story problem.

> Finding missing factors can give children valuable calculating and estimating experiences.

3. How could this array model help someone solve 5×4?

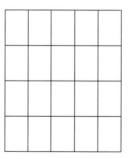

Could you solve 4×5 using the same model? Why or why not?
   Show an array for 13×8. Write and solve a story problem based on this model.

> Asking children about commutativity in relationship to their story problems can lead to an interesting class conversation. Is 8 by 13 the same as 13 by 8? Sometimes it is and sometimes it is not, depending on the context.

4. Calculate the solutions to these multiplication problems. How can you explain the pattern you can use to find the products when multiplying by zeros?

$$20 \times 300 = \_\_ \qquad 500 \times 500 = \_\_$$
$$60 \times 80 = \_\_ \qquad 4 \times 900 = \_\_$$
$$100 \times 800 = \_\_ \qquad 20 \times 80 = \_\_$$

How could you adjust your explanation to articulate the pattern you notice when completing these calculations?

$$30 \times 18 = \_\_ \qquad 343 \times 90 = \_\_$$
$$53 \times 80 = \_\_ \qquad 24 \times 400 = \_\_$$
$$118 \times 40 = \_\_ \qquad 123 \times 300 = \_\_$$

As students work to make sense of the multiplication process, it becomes increasingly important for their shortcuts to be grounded in understanding. Articulating patterns and justifying shortcuts will help students better understand why and how multiplication works.

Questions 5, 6, and 7 follow a possible progression of teaching and thinking in order to help children make sense of multidigit multiplication. It can be helpful for students to discover important multiplicative principles as they work to solve problems. The ability to identify and generalize patterns will support their learning and help them articulate why multiplication works as it does. Each question could take a period—or a week! Valuable multiplication practice will occur as students work to explain and support their solutions, particularly when asked, "Will this work for all groups of numbers?" You may need to make instructional decisions about the amount of time you want to spend on these questions.

5. How could you break apart 235 to make 235×7 a simpler problem? Would that work for any number? Explain and support your reasoning with other examples.

$$235 \times 7 = (200 \times 7) + (30 \times 7) + (5 \times 7)$$

Students can easily lose sight of the necessity of preserving place value when multiplying. Activities that require students to decompose numbers remind them of the magnitude of each single digit within a larger number.

6. Reproduce this array on graph paper.

Using colored pencils, how could you prove that 14 × 23 = (10 × 20) + (10 × 3) + (4 × 20) + (4 × 3)?

It is important that students in the fifth and sixth grades be able to make sense of multidigit multiplications. The multiplications involved in multidigit multiplication are not random!

Array models allow students to visually decompose factors to make for friendlier, perhaps more manageable, multiplications.

There will be those students who will find this model of multiplication and this type of activity powerful. The ability to decompose factors becomes visible and meaningful.

Activities such as this can lead students to important discoveries and understandings about the distributive property. Asking students to apply their proofs to other multiplication problems will allow them to make important generalizations. Asking a follow-up question such as "Will this work with all two-digit numbers?" will give students additional opportunities to apply the distributive property.

7. How could you break apart each factor to make 46 × 58 an easier problem? What problem could you start with? How could you make sure you had completed all the multiplications required by this problem? Will this work for every two-digit multiplication problem?

An understanding of number sense, place value, and the application of the distributive property is necessary in the construction of a partial-products algorithm.

Good Questions for Math Teaching

There are several procedures that could be employed, such as $58 \times 46 = (50 + 8) \times (40 + 6)$.

There will be four multiplications:

50×40
50×6
8×40
8×6

Changing the factors to 60×46 is also a possibility. Some interesting and valuable understandings, as well as misconceptions, about how to handle those two extra 46s can come about using this strategy. Since we have added two extra 46s, now what do we do with them to get back to our original problem?

The application of and generalizations made about the distributive property are more important than the recitation of the property itself at the fifth- and sixth-grade levels.

8. Study the progression of factors and products. How does each equation build upon the equation that precedes it?

$6 \times 7 = 42$ $5 \times 9 = 45$
$60 \times 7 = 420$ $5 \times 90 = 450$
$60 \times 14 = 840$ $5 \times 45 = 225$
$30 \times 14 = 420$ $50 \times 45 = 2{,}250$
$15 \times 14 = 210$ $25 \times 45 = 1{,}125$

The prealgebraic concept of balance, or equivalence, can begin to develop from these sequences and questions. If a factor is doubled, then so too is the product. If a product is halved, then so is one of the factors. The visual image of keeping both sides of an equation balanced is very helpful to fifth and sixth graders.

Creating these sequences is extremely helpful for both teachers and students. It gives all of us the opportunity to mentally play with factors and products.

9. Using the numbers 1, 2, 3, and 4:

Create the *largest* product by filling in the blanks:

_ _ × _ _   _ _ _ × _

Create the *smallest* product by filling in the blanks:

$$\_\_ \times \_\_ \qquad\qquad \_\_\_ \times \_$$

How does the order of the digits affect the product?

> Applying discovered generalizations can strengthen multiplicative thinking, estimating, and problem solving.
>
> Problems such as these often create valuable calculating practice.
>
> Additional questions using the numbers 5, 6, 7, and 8 could also be constructed to support generalizations.

10. Which of the following problems has the largest product? Try to figure it out by solving as few problems as possible. How did you choose which problems to do or not do?

42 × 17	24 × 12	52 × 11
40 × 20	50 × 24	43 × 16
36 × 36	12 × 14	42 × 42

> Although this looks like a question about calculation, it is perhaps more about place value, estimation, and the effects of multiplication.
>
> Listening to students' strategies as they explain which problems they chose to do or not to do gives teachers valuable insights as to how students think about numbers and what happens to their magnitude when they are multiplied.

11. Write a story about what life might be like if suddenly something became "ten times more." For example, what would life be like if your math teacher gave you ten times more math homework a night? Or what would life be like if mosquitoes were ten times as big? Use your imagination, but be specific. Give counts or measurements to support your story.

> At this age, students are beginning to encounter multiplicative comparison situations but have some difficulty knowing what to do with them! Writing a story can create a visual image as well as reinforce the magnitude of multiplication by ten.
>
> Follow-up division stories could be written within the context of ten times less. What would life be like if math class were ten times shorter? What would life be like if you suddenly became ten times smaller?

12. Dee Vide wanted to solve 568/8 and 2,306/6 in this way:

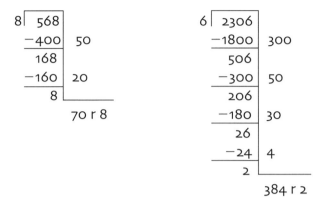

How does this method of division work? Why does it make sense? What could you name this procedure? Could you think of other ways to solve these problems?

> This partial-products division algorithm has begun to be a procedure of choice for many young mathematicians because the dividend remains a complete number, even after the subtractions. Students are often more quickly able to make sense of this procedure and of the division involved than of the standard algorithm.

13. Mrs. Candrive's class has been collecting aluminum cans to recycle. Her first-period class has collected a total of 504 cans. There are twenty-four students in her class. How many cans has each student collected if each student collected an equal amount? Give a written explanation to justify your solution.

> This division situation can be classified as *partitive*. We know how many groups into which to divide the cans (twenty-four groups). What we do not know is how many objects (cans) are in each group.

14. Mrs. Candrive's class continues to collect aluminum cans to recycle. Each child in her third-period class has collected about 12 cans each. The third-period class has collected 312 cans total. How many students are in the third-period class? Give a written explanation to justify your solution.

> This division situation can be classified as *quotative*. In quotative division situations, the number of objects (cans) in each group is known, but the number of groups (number of students) is not.
>
> It is important to include division situations that require both partitive and quotative manipulation in instruction. If children are presented with just one division situation, they will find it difficult to make sense of the other.

15. Solve this sequence of story problems:

- Twenty-five fifth graders are going to the Red Sox game. Four fifth graders can be seated in one car. How many cars will be needed to get the fifth graders to Fenway Park?
- Howard, a baseball fanatic, has $25 in his pocket. Red Sox pennants cost $4 each. How many pennants can Howard buy?
- Remember Howard? He still has $25 in his pocket. And he still wants to buy pennants that cost $4 each. How much money will he have left to put toward a Fenway Frank (hot dog) if he buys six pennants?
- Howard decided not to buy the pennants. Who needs six pennants anyway? And he still has that $25. Howard realizes he can buy four baseballs instead. How much does each baseball cost?

How is each story problem the same? How are they different? In what way does the remainder affect the solution of each problem?

Remainders happen! Context gives children the opportunity to determine what should be done with a remainder. Should it

- cause the quotient to be rounded up to the next whole number (as in the first solution)?
- be ignored (as in the second solution)?
- be the solution to the problem (as in the third solution)?
- be written as a fraction or a decimal (as in the fourth solution)?

Students will quickly realize that the number model for each story problem is the same. What they may not realize right away is how the remainder determines the solution.

The importance of carefully reading story problems and understanding what is being asked is often overlooked by students and teachers alike. In this particular context, the reading becomes as important as the arithmetic.

It is always possible to change the context to fit a particular class or geographic area. If the Red Sox context does not work for you or your students, try changing the sports team or city to fit your needs.

Students may enjoy creating their own story problem sequences such as the one in this question. Choosing simple division number models can set the stage for wonderfully creative story problems. Having students share and categorize problems as to how the remainder is used can help them strengthen important understandings about solutions derived from division.

16. Write a story problem for 127/5. Solve your story problem. Does your answer have a remainder? How do you know? If there is a remainder, what are you going to do with it?

> Writing story problems that match division expressions can be difficult for fifth and sixth graders. Their understanding of how to apply the division process can be fragile.
>
> If a student presents a "wrong" story problem, it is helpful to rework the problem as a class in order to make it fit the expression. Class conversations can help identify misconceptions and move children toward increased understanding of how division works.
>
> If students have some fluency with divisibility rules, they will realize that this problem will have a remainder without computation because 127 is not divisible by 5.

17. Create a division story problem whose solution has a remainder of eighteen. How does the remainder affect your solution? How did you think through this problem?

> Problems with missing divisors and dividends can offer additional calculating and estimation practice. Children may try several division problems (or multiplication problems) and develop estimation strategies in order to adhere to the constraints of the problem.

18. Are the answers below correct? If you think an answer is incorrect, tell whether the given answer is too large or too small. *Then* calculate to see if you were correct.

$$\frac{8,638}{7} = 123.4 \qquad \frac{5,076}{9} = 564$$

$$\frac{696}{8} = 5,568 \qquad \frac{6,785}{5} = 1,357$$

$$\frac{2,428}{4} = 67 \qquad \frac{2,961}{6} = 49.35$$

> Assessing the reasonableness of an answer can at times be more helpful than finding the solution. Sharing strategies can help children validate their thinking, number sense, and understanding of division.

19. What three-digit number can be divisible by two, five, and ten? Explain your thinking.

Multiplication and Proportional Reasoning

Questions such as this relate to students' ability to apply and manipulate divisibility rules.

A question that has an unlimited number of solutions quickly engages children. Not only will children find numbers that work, but they will also discover numbers that will not work and why. Encourage children to question their answers!

The solution needs to be even (divisible by two), and it must end with a zero (divisible by ten, which also means it is divisible by five).

Possible solutions include 180 and 770.

20. What three- (or four- or five- or six- . . .) digit number can be divisible by two, three, five, and six? Explain your thinking.

Solutions need to be

- even (divisible by two)
- divisible by three (the sum of the digits is divisible by three)
- divisible by six (if the number is divisible by two *and* three, then it is also divisible by six)
- divisible by five (the number ends in five or zero)

Possible solutions include 150 and 330.

Post students' answers. Ask students if their numbers meet the given criteria. Do students realize that all of their numbers are also divisible by thirty? Why is that so?

21. What four- (or five- or six- . . .) digit number can be divisible by two, six, and nine? Explain your thinking.

Solutions need to be

- even (divisible by two)
- divisible by three (to be divisible by six, the number needs to be divisible by two and three)
- divisible by nine (the sum of the digits is divisible by nine)

Possible solutions include 6,372 and 1,206.

22. Green Giant Fertilizer and water are mixed in the ratio of one part fertilizer to two parts water. Complete the chart below.

Fertilizer	100 ml	25 ml	?	1.5 L	?	?
Water	200 ml	?	250 ml	?	4 L	490 ml

If you have 410 ml of water in your sprayer and 115 ml of Green Giant Fertilizer left in the original container, can you make a full-strength solution? If you cannot, will the solution be weaker or stronger than it needs to be? How much more water or fertilizer would you need to make a full-strength solution?

Determining the proportional relationship between a divisor and a dividend can be helpful when children are working to make sense of the division process.

Questions that require children to identify proportional relationships between two quantities can help support and develop this reasoning skill.

Asking students about the weakness or strength of the solution pushes their understanding of the numerical relationships.

23. Use the information in Column A to help you complete the other columns.

	A	B	C	D
Sugar	16 oz.	32 oz.	?	14 oz.
Flour	4 oz.	?	7 oz.	?

What is ratio of sugar to flour? _____ : _____

Decomposing divisors and dividends into smaller, "friendlier" numbers depends upon a student's ability to think about numbers and their proportional relationship to each other.

24. A 32-gram serving of Cinnamon Life contains 9 grams of sugar. A 55-gram serving of Raisin Nut Bran contains 16 grams of sugar. (Both are ¾ cup servings.) Which cereal has less sugar per gram of cereal? How do you know?

Answering this question could present challenges as well as many different strategies! The problem presented is not the same as in Questions 22 and 23. Students are being asked to compare two different proportions, which extends the thinking required in the previous two questions.

Looking at ratios and playing around with relative equivalence can be helpful for this particular question. The division is not particularly difficult. It is the interpretation of that division that can be powerful.

Multiplication and Proportional Reasoning

Grades 7–8

EXPERIENCES AT THIS LEVEL WILL HELP STUDENTS TO

- recognize multiplicative and proportional reasoning in real-world situations
- write part-to-part and part-to-whole ratios and rates using different notations
- use the language associated with ratios
- represent proportional relationships using words, pictures, tables, and numbers
- set up and solve proportions

MATERIALS

- calculators
- rulers

Good Questions and Teacher Notes

1. Count the numbers of males and females in this class. Write as many ratios as you can about this information.

> Encourage students to write both part-to-part and part-to-whole ratios using both colon and fraction bar notation. Students should also interpret each ratio they write using phrases associated with ratios.

2. Last year, the Salem Sluggers won nine out of every thirteen games. Kristina thinks this means that they won nine in a row and then lost four in a row. Do you agree or disagree? Why?

> This question confronts the misconception that the comparison of games won to those played describes the games *consecutively*. To help students with this misconception, ask them to describe a sequence of wins and losses in a twenty-six-game season that results in a nine-to-thirteen ratio. Students will see that varying orders of wins and losses can result in the given ratio.

3. A vase holds red and white roses only. For every three red roses, there are two white roses. How many flowers might be in the vase?

> A common misconception is that there must be only five flowers in the vase. The ratio 3:2 can actually be repeated any integral number of times for any total amount of flowers that is a multiple of five.

Good Questions for Math Teaching

4. A movie rental store has movies on both DVD and videotape. The store has six times as many movies on DVD as on videotape. What fraction of the movies might be on DVD?

> The statement given in the question compares the part of the movies that are on DVD with the part that are on videotape. In order to answer the question asked, students will need to translate this part-to-part comparison into a fraction comparing a part with the whole.

5. Florida grapefruits are on sale for three for $1.45. One dozen California grapefruits offer a better buy. How much might the California grapefruits cost?

> Comparing and contrasting students' solution methods will help them generalize the proportionality that is present in all methods.

6. Approximately 11 percent of the population is left-handed. Use this information to estimate the total number of lefties in this school.

> Instead of telling students how many students are in the school, encourage students to use proportional reasoning to estimate the number of students in the school (e.g., number of students in their class times the number of classes in their grade times the number of grades in the school).

7. The population density of Larry's town is 212.4 people per square mile. The town is 5 square miles in area. How many people might actually live in each square mile?

> Students sometimes have the misconception that population density represents the actual number of people per square mile as opposed to the average number of people per square mile. Answering this question will help them make this distinction.

8. The athletic director in the town of Hingham kept track of the number of students who signed up to play intermural basketball, soccer, and volleyball. He looked at the sign-up lists and made these conclusions: "The number of students interested in playing basketball is about three times greater than the number of students interested in playing soccer. Two out of every five students signed up to play basketball." How many students might have signed up for each sport?

> Once students find quantities that satisfy the athletic director's conclusions, ask students to use ratios and comparative language to make other conclusions.

Multiplication and Proportional Reasoning

9. Claire made a scale drawing of a large banner she plans to create for the school pep rally. The measurements for the length and the width of the banner will actually contain fractions, but she chose a scale so that the drawing had whole number measurements. What might have been the scale Claire used? Using this scale, what might have been the measurements of Claire's drawing and the measurements of the actual banner?

> One way to engage students in a discussion of this question is to ask a student to reveal his or her answers to the first two parts of this question and then ask the rest of the class to figure out what that student's answer to the third part must be.

10. A friend of mine walks an 18-minute mile. How many miles per hour must I walk in order to walk faster than her?

> This question helps students make sense of and compare two common unit rates—minutes per mile and miles per hour.

11. During a road race, Runner A ran 12 miles in 1 hour and 20 minutes. Runner B ran 15 miles in $2\frac{1}{2}$ hours. Runner C ran faster than Runner A but slower than Runner B. What might Runner C's speed have been?

> Do students realize that they need to convert the times to either minutes or hours?

12. Last year, the ratio of girls to boys at Camp Brady was three to one. How would enrollment have to change in order for the ratio to be one to two?

> Drawing a picture of the ratio and then adapting that picture to create the new ratio is an effective way of answering this question. Insist that students give a quantitative answer and not a qualitative one such as "More boys need to enroll." For eaxample, there would be one girl enrolled for every two boys enrolled if the number of girls remained constant but the number of boys grew by six times. Or for every one additional girl that enrolls, seven additional boys must enroll.

13. Sarintino's restaurant advertises that it offers two food servers for every nine guests. Zapoteka restaurant seats 135 guests and boasts a better food-server-to-guest ratio. How many food servers might it have?

> Since the ratio 2:9 equates to 30:135, students need to realize that Zapoteka needs *more than* thirty food servers.

14. The ratio of cats to dogs in a neighborhood is exactly 2.4 to 1. How many cats and how many dogs might be in this neighborhood?

> In addition to sharing students' answers, discuss what the ratio 2.4 cats to 1 dog really means. Do students understand that this ratio conveys that there are almost two and a half times as many cats as dogs?

15. Chip-a-Choo Cookie Company boasts "1,000 chips in every bag!" How could we determine whether this claim is true without counting the chips in every cookie?

> One strategy is to take a sample of cookies, finding the average number of chips in that sample, and then multiplying the average by the total number of cookies in the bag.

16. Mrs. Kilban drove 30 miles in 1 hour at *varying* speeds. Describe the different speeds she might have driven at, how long she traveled at them, and how far she got while driving at each speed.

> While miles per hour is a common unit rate, in reality speeds are rarely maintained for a full hour. As a result, students need as much experience scaling *down* unit rates as they do scaling them up.

7 Fractions, Decimals, and Percents

The National Council of Teachers of Mathematics (2000) proposes that middle grades students develop a deep understanding of rational number concepts, become proficient in rational number computation and estimation, and learn to think flexibly about relationships among fractions, decimals, and percents. Carefully crafted questions can help support our students as they work toward conceptual and procedural understanding of rational numbers.

Fractions (Grades 5–6)

EXPERIENCES AT THIS LEVEL WILL HELP CHILDREN TO

- use different forms of representations such as physical models and drawings to reason about situations requiring the manipulation of fractions
- compare and order fractions
- use benchmarks that relate different forms of representations of rational numbers
- explore addition, subtraction, multiplication, and division of fractions
- use estimation to help make decisions
- develop methods for solving problems involving fractions

MATERIALS

- construction paper
- Cuisenaire rods

- fractions dot paper (see Blackline Masters)
- pattern blocks
- pattern block templates
- pattern block figure (see Blackline Masters)
- 6-by-6-inch template (see Blackline Masters)
- scissors

Much time is spent studying fractions, decimals, and percents in the fifth and sixth grades. It has become increasingly evident that fractions, decimals, and percents are too often manipulated by rote by both teachers and students rather than by conceptual and procedural understandings. Many of the following questions concentrate on the construction of meaningful procedures and strategies supported by conceptual understandings. Often students perceive fractions and decimals as two separate units of study. Their equivalence and interchangablity are often overlooked as we rush to teach computational skills. Whenever possible, symbolically represent decimals as fractions ($0.25 = \frac{25}{100}$). When speaking of decimals, using the language of "tenths" or "hundredths" instead of "point five" or "point twenty-five" can help students make the important connections between decimals and fractions. Weaving percents into our classroom conversations, activities, and questions can also help students make the necessary connections between fractional, decimal, and percentage notation and representation. Using language such as "per hundred" or "for every hundred" when discussing percents can be helpful for students as they move from one representation to another.

Some teachers may feel that some of these questions will be too easy for their students. Students can often manipulate fractions, find common denominators, and solve addition and subtraction problems without context with apparent ease. We also find, however, that the rote manipulation of fractions cannot compensate for a lack of understanding of fractional relationships. There will frequently be that handful of students who resist this type of instruction and questioning because they believe that they have mastered the given procedure. Asking students to justify their reasoning and to prove their answers whether with models or symbolic representations becomes increasingly important as we help students construct computational proficiency, efficiency, and understanding. It is equally important to construct questions that will allow students opportunities to formulate understandings about how fractions work. Many times students will begin a lesson with one understanding only to find that it needs to be readjusted and reevaluated as the lesson continues, given the nature of the activities and questions being asked.

Good Questions and Teacher Notes: Pattern Block Fractions

1. If the $\triangle = 1$, what is the value of the following shape? [See Blackline Masters.]

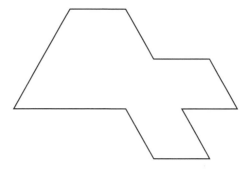

If the $\triangle = \frac{1}{4}$, what is the value of the preceding shape?
If the $\triangle = \frac{1}{2}$, what is the value of the preceding shape *now?*

Why do the same shapes keep switching values? Explain your reasoning with tracings of the pattern blocks and/or other diagrams.

> Because of the given contexts (the value of the $\triangle$), the value of the whole changes. This can be a very difficult and eye-opening concept for budding fraction aficionados! The whole matters. Understanding and being able to represent the whole becomes increasingly important as students are asked to make sense of their interpretations.
>
> Pattern blocks are only one model that can be used to represent this big idea when studying fractions. (See the next section for a model question using Cuisenaire rods.)

2. If the blue rhombus equals $\frac{1}{4}$, create a shape with a value of $2\frac{1}{4}$. Sketch your construction and label each fractional part. Write an addition sentence that matches your construction on a sentence strip. Post the construction and turn in your addition sentence.

> Once the constructions and sentences have been completed, hold up an addition sentence and have the students match the sentence to its construction. This valuable exercise will reinforce the need for students to write what they see.
>
> Repeat this activity choosing different shapes and assigning different values. Make sure to try them out first yourself!

Good Questions and Teacher Notes: Cuisenaire Rods

1. If the dark green rod equals 1, what is the value of the following rods? Defend your position using the rods and what you know about fractional relationships.

red = _____   light green = _____   white = _____

Make trains of these rods (see diagram below) and place them in front of you to help support your positions.

Dark Green					
Green			Green		
Red		Red		Red	
W	W	W	W	W	W

Create new trains as your value of the whole changes in order to answer the following questions:

orange = 1	brown = 1	orange + red = 1
red =	red =	red =
yellow =	purple =	light green =
white =	white =	dark green =
		white =

As with the first pattern block activity in the preceding section, this activity provides students with another model as they investigate the meaning of a whole and how that meaning impacts the naming of fractional parts.

The visual model of the rods enables students to begin to reason about the relative size of fractional parts as well: that thirds are smaller than halves, fourths are larger than eighths, and so on.

As we teach for understanding, it is important to ask students to justify the thinking behind their statements. For example, *Why* do you think the red rod is one-half? *Why* is the red rod one-half in this problem and not one-half in another problem?

Good Questions and Teacher Notes: Fraction Kit (Burns 2000, 226)

1. Create your own fraction kit out of construction paper with halves, fourths, and sixteenths. What are the various strings of fractions that can add up to one whole? Can you find strings of three fractions? Four fractions? Five fractions? What is the longest string you can find that will add up to one whole? What is the shortest string? Write your strings as addition sentences.

The fraction kit offers yet another model for seeing fractional parts and representations.

Writing strings ($\frac{1}{2} + \frac{1}{4} + \frac{1}{4} = 1$) offers students the opportunity to symbolically represent fractions.

Informal conjectures about how adding works with fractions will also begin to develop when working with these strings.

Adding strings of unlike denominators also gives students the opportunity to think through the numerical relationships of the given denominators. How are two, four, eight, and sixteen related? What is the relationship of the numerator to the denominator?

 Because these fraction kits are so portable, homework assignments can easily be based on their usage.

2. Using fractions dot paper [see Blackline Masters], how many ways can you divide each square into fourths?

Students will quickly divide the whole into the common divisions of fourths. Instructional conversations will quickly ensue once the topic of irregular fourths, or shapes, is introduced, either by the teacher or by a student example.

Are the pieces fourths if they do not look the same? can be a powerful question. Would each person get an equal amount if we were dividing up a pan of brownies? What constitutes equal?

Encourage students to develop and articulate their strategies and reasoning for proving that noncongruent shapes can be equal. Show them the following diagram and ask: "Is this a fair division? How do you know?"

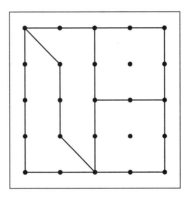

Using an area model, each region constitutes $\frac{1}{4}$.

$\frac{1}{4}$ of 16 units^2 = 4 units^2

Each region equals 4 units^2.

 Asking students to work with eighths within this same model can be an insightful follow-up activity in order to assess understanding and progress.

3. Use a 6-by-6-inch template [see Blackline Masters] to answer the following questions: How can you divide this square into halves, fourths, *and* eighths? Is there more than one way to divide up your square? Show your thinking on your diagram. Partition your square into halves, fourths, and eighths. Label and color-code each fractional part. Justify your divisions and labels.

> Such an activity becomes more difficult without the use of dot paper. Rulers and even cutting out and folding the square can be useful. When students use rulers, rich conversations can develop around how to measure one-half of 3 inches or one-fourth of 6 inches.
>
> EXTENSION   This same activity can be used to investigate and represent thirds, sixths, and twelfths.

4. $\frac{1}{2} = \frac{2}{3}$

Is this equation true or false? Support your thinking given any model discussed in class.

> Extending the use of such a question using other familiar fractions can solidify understanding. Have students articulate their reasoning in writing with the aid of diagrams as well as in a class discussion.
>
> Using unfamiliar fractions can develop new understandings based on what the students have already discovered about fractional parts. For example:
>
> $\frac{1}{15} < \frac{1}{16}$ *True or false? Why?*

5. What patterns can you see in this series? How is each fraction related to the others? What do you notice about the third term? What do you notice about the fifth term? Can you predict the eleventh term?

$$\{ \tfrac{1}{3}, \tfrac{2}{6}, \tfrac{3}{9}, \tfrac{4}{12}, \tfrac{5}{15}, \cdots \}$$

> Yes, these fractions are equivalent, but ask students to identify relationships between the fractions. Students may see the following:
>
> ■ As the numerator increases by one, the denominator increases by three.
> ■ The numerator increases more "slowly" than the denominator.
> ■ The third term has 3 as a numerator; the fifth term has 5; the eleventh term will have 11 as the numerator.
>
> EXTENSION   Initially, choose patterns that begin with the *unit fraction* (a fraction with a numerator of one). Moving on to patterns that start with fractions other than the unit fraction will help further develop students' understanding of *how* equivalent fractions can be generated and *how* they relate to one another.

6. $\frac{1}{2}$ $\frac{5}{12}$ $\frac{1}{4}$ $\frac{8}{10}$ $\frac{2}{3}$

Who am I?

Clues:

> I am less than one-half.
> I am greater than one-third.
> My denominator is a multiple of three.
> I am simplified.
> I am _____.

Make up a fraction riddle with five fractions and clues for identifying one of them.

> A student's ability to compare and contrast fractions can demonstrate conceptual as well as procedural understanding. Creating riddles also allows students the opportunity to apply other numerical concepts to their clues.

Good Questions and Teacher Notes: Adding and Subtracting Fractions

1. Write a story problem that can be solved with this number sentence:

$$2\frac{1}{4} + \frac{1}{8} + 1\frac{1}{2} = 3\frac{7}{8}$$

Justify its solution as well. Use visual models *and* number sentences.

> Writing story problems can help teachers assess students' understanding or misconceptions. We can assess how the students are adding but also how they are making sense of the fractional relationships within the context of their stories.
>
> Asking students to write about subtraction models is as important as having them write about addition models.

2. If you add me to three-fourths, you end up with seven-eighths. What fractional part am I? Demonstrate your solution with a visual model and/or number sentence. Can you demonstrate another way of solving this riddle?

> Students who have a good understanding of fractional relationships can very often be flexible in their thinking; for example, $\frac{3}{4} + ? = \frac{7}{8}$ or $\frac{7}{8} - \frac{3}{4} = ?$
>
> Fractional riddles such as this can help students apply what they already know about whole number operations to what they are learning about fractions.
>
> The formation of riddles can easily be applied to decimals, or even to both decimals and fractions in one riddle!

Fractions, Decimals, and Percents

3. Using the digits 1 through 8, place one digit in each box to satisfy the following: What is the least possible sum? What is the greatest possible sum? How did you go about making your number choices?

$$\frac{\square}{\square} + \frac{\square}{\square}$$

> This question not only asks students to add fractions but also to make judgments about the relative value of each fraction created. Students must also consider relationships between the numerators and denominators when placing the digits.

4. $\frac{1}{a} - \frac{1}{b} = \frac{1}{c}$

Find three different numbers for the denominators that will make this a true sentence. Can you find another set of numbers that will work?

> Initially, students may employ a guess-and-check procedure. Some students will also be convinced that this sentence will be false no matter what numbers are chosen. Asking students to focus on common denominators can help open up thinking and reasoning. Once students have decided on a set of numbers, have them test their fractions within the given equation. Calculation practice takes on meaning and purpose when presented in a problem-solving context.

Good Questions and Teacher Notes: Multiplication and Division of Fractions

1. [Draw seven circles on the board.] If you had seven cookies to divide up among four people, how could you do it? How many cookies—or what part of a cookie—would each person get? Write your solution as an addition fraction string that equals seven.

> Answering this question in a whole-class format can be of great help to the students. They can tell you how to divide the cookies, and you can demonstrate the division on the board.
>
> It is important for the students to represent their divisions symbolically. Initially, it may not be a formalized number sentence. Partitioning cookies and then labeling their parts is a common and very helpful approach. Ask students to formalize their solutions into number sentences once they have made sense of their divisions and reasons for doing so.
>
> Students should be encouraged to prove their thinking and to justify their reasoning to you, each other, and/or in writing.

EXTENSION   Share four cookies with six people. Share eight cookies with five people. Dividing brownies (squares) can give students another model with which to test their procedures and understanding.

2. I have twenty-four coins in my pocket.

- ■ One-half of the coins are quarters.
- ■ One-fourth of the coins are dimes.
- ■ One-eighth of the coins are nickels.
- ■ One-eighth of the coins are pennies.

How much money do I have in my pocket? How did you come to this conclusion? Describe your thinking. How would you have changed your procedure if the amount of money were known and you were asked how many coins I had in my pocket?

Multiple manipulations are necessary in solving coin riddles such as these. There are also multiple methods of finding solutions, which makes these riddles interesting and entertaining to process. Some may utilize a guess-and-check procedure and others may opt for an algebraic computation method.

EXTENSION   Having students make up their own riddles, as well as describing their procedures for creating and solving them, can be a useful extension. It may be necessary to model how to devise a coin riddle as a class activity, keeping in mind that the fractional parts listed need to be components of one whole (the amount of money or the number of coins). It is not an easy procedure!

3. Annie is a great baby-sitter. She makes $6.50 an hour. Dava is an even better baby-sitter. She makes $2\frac{1}{2}$ times more than Annie per hour.

How much does Dava make per hour?

How much more does Dava make than Annie per hour?

How many hours does Annie need to baby-sit before she can equal Dava's pay for two hours of baby-sitting?

The relational language in multiplicative comparison problems (*times as many, times more*) is difficult for many students. Students will often decide to add or subtract, confusing *times more* with *more than*. Presenting story problems based on relational comparisons will help students identify the appropriate operation.

Problems that include both fractions and decimals present contextual situations that require students to make problem-solving choices. Can the student manipulate both in the same problem? Is it necessary to convert one to the

Fractions, Decimals, and Percents

other? Which form makes more sense given the context—or does it really matter which form is used?

4. Can you find a fraction and a whole number with a product that is a whole number? Can you find a fraction and a whole number with a product less than one-half? Can you find a fraction and a whole number with a product greater than one? Can you find a fraction and a whole number with a product greater than one and one-half but less than two? Explain your method for choosing and checking possible solutions.

> Questions such as these can offer students more meaningful calculation practice than a sheet of multiplication problems! Reasoning skills, as well as procedural proficiency, are necessary to test and identify solutions. You may also find that students will complete many more calculations as they search for fractions and whole numbers that will produce the desired products.
>
> Asking students to test solutions offered by you or student volunteers can also provide further calculating practice.

5. When you multiply two whole numbers, the product is larger than the factors. When is the product of two fractions smaller than the fractions being multiplied? Explain your reasoning and give examples to support your thinking.

> When multiplying fractions that are less than one, you are taking a part of something that itself is part of a whole. The product can, therefore, *not* be bigger than either of the two fractions. This can be very confusing to students who have come to believe that multiplication makes something bigger.

6. When dividing fractions, can your answer be greater than, less than, or between the two fractions you are dividing? Explain why or why not for each situation and give examples to illustrate your position.

> The answer to all three is yes, which will surprise many students. Some will automatically assume that the answer will always be *less than* the original fractions because to divide is often equated with making something smaller.
>
> It may be necessary for you to model a situation for each solution, but it will be well worth the time. Not all students will walk away saying, "Oh yes, I see." At the very least, students will walk away with an understanding that dividing with fractions does not always denote making them smaller.
>
> The answer can be *greater* than the fractions you are dividing: $\frac{3}{4} \div \frac{1}{4} = 3$, which means that there are three one-fourths in three-fourths.
>
> The answer can be *smaller* than the fractions you are dividing: $\frac{3}{4} \div 2 = \frac{3}{8}$. Dividing a fraction by a whole number is the same as multiplying it by its

Good Questions for Math Teaching

reciprocal. The reciprocal is a number less than one, which brings us back to the question of what happens when you multiply two fractions.

The answer can be *in between*: $\frac{1}{4} \div \frac{3}{4} = \frac{1}{3}$. If the problem is rewritten with common denominators, the relationship is easier to see: $\frac{3}{12} \div \frac{4}{12} = \frac{9}{12}$.

7. Suppose that Max, the wonder dog, ate one-third of a bag of doggie treats on Sunday night. Max then proceeded to eat one-fourth of what remained in the bag every night after that. How many nights would it take until the bag was half gone? Could you determine when it would be time to buy Max another bag of doggie treats? Draw a diagram to support your solutions.

Using array diagrams can be helpful to students as they work to determine when the bag was half gone. The bag would be half gone by Monday night.

Mon.	Mon.	Sun.
		Sun.
		Sun.
		Sun.

After Monday, six out of the
twelve parts are gone.

Responses to the second question (when will it be time to buy another bag?) is subject to the individual opinions of the students. Will the bag ever be empty? Can you theoretically ever have an empty bag if you are forever taking one-quarter of what is left?

This problem can also be reworked using percentages. In that case, a pie chart may be a better visual representation.

Decimals (Grades 5–6)

EXPERIENCES AT THIS LEVEL WILL HELP CHILDREN TO

■ use different forms of representations such as physical models and drawings to reason about situations requiring the manipulation of decimal numbers

■ compare and order decimals

■ use benchmarks that relate different representations of rational numbers

- explore addition, subtraction, multiplication, and division of decimal numbers
- use estimation to make decisions
- develop methods for solving problems involving fractions and decimal numbers

MATERIALS

- tenths and hundredths grid (see Blackline Masters)
- hundredths grid (see Blackline Masters)
- meter sticks, decimeters, centimeter cubes (orange and white Cuisenaire rods work well)

Good Questions and Teacher Notes

1. Decide whether each decimal is closer to zero, one-half, or one. Shade in the decimal amounts on a tenths or hundredths grid to justify your thinking [see Blackline Masters].

    0.29   0.55   0.03   0.4   0.09   0.90   0.6   0.75

Benchmark decimals and fractions can serve as useful reference points. Being able to identify the relative value of decimals can help students make better comparisons between decimals and fractions.

Asking the follow-up question "How do you know?" once an answer is given allows the teacher to hear students' understandings or misconceptions.

You may also want to add one-fourth and three-fourths to your benchmarks as students become more comfortable with this activity. *They* may also ask to include these benchmarks!

2. Mrs. Flo Wer is planting a garden. She wants to follow the plans below.

Flo wants four-tenths of the garden to be planted with geraniums.

Flo wants fifteen-hundredths of the garden to be planted with marigolds.

Flo wants three-tenths of the garden to be planted with tulips.

Flo wants the remaining sections of her garden to be planted with sunflowers and daisies.

Use a hundredths grid to "plant" Mrs. Flo Wer's garden [see Blackline Masters]. Complete the chart with the fraction and decimal equivalent of the garden space that will be allotted to each kind of flower in your plan.

Flower	Fraction	Decimal

Adding a column for percent notation is also a possibility. This type of visual model lends itself well to a discussion of percent.

 Why do some students' gardens look different than others? Are they "correct," given Flo's requirements? Explain your position.

3. Using these units of measure:

    meter stick
    decimeter
    centimeter
    (meter = 1 whole)

How could you represent 2.17? How could you represent 0.9? How could you represent 0.28? What place value does the meter stick represent? The deci-meter? The centimeter cube? Using these measures, how can you prove that 0.3 = 0.30? What would one-thousandth look like?

This measurement model can be helpful when students are working to make sense of the multiplicative relationship between decimal place values. Defining the root *deci-* of *decimal* can also help highlight the relationship.

4. Where do the following decimals fit? How do you know?

    0.86   0.2   0.99   0.49   0.75   0.01   0.6

    0 — — — — — —0.5— — — — — — 1.0

It is important to give students multiple opportunities to talk about order and equivalence in regard to decimals. Having access to tenths and hundredths grid paper may be helpful to some as they explain their thinking.

 Add in fractions!

5. Mark and label a point for a decimal number that fits each description below.

1 —————————————————————— 2

a point close to, but larger than 1
a point close to, but smaller than $1\frac{1}{2}$
a point close to, but larger than $1\frac{1}{2}$
a point close to, but smaller than 2

As with fractions, it is important for students to see decimals in multiple representations. Using number lines can offer students a continuum on which to see quantity and equivalence.

6. Solve this riddle.

1 _._ _ _

Clue 1: The digit in the hundredths place is double the digit in the tenths place.

Clue 2: The digit in the tenths place is odd.

Clue 3: The digit in the thousandths place represents the sum of the digits in the tenths place and hundredths place.

Clue 4: The digit in the tenths place represents the sum of the digits in the hundredths place and the thousandths place.

Clue 5: The digit in the ones place is four times the digit in the hundredths place.

Number riddles can provide a context within which to review and solidify place value understandings. The spelling alone (adding the ever important *-ths* to decimal places) of the place values is important!

EXTENSION   Have students make up their own riddles.

7. True or false?

$\frac{1}{2} = 0.5$

Are these two quantities *equal* or *equivalent?* How do you know? Justify your thinking with a diagram or drawing.

> Some may argue that these two specific *written representations* are not equal because they do not look the same. They do, however, represent the same *value,* which makes them equivalent. This idea of equivalence is extremely important in the study of mathematics. Conversations around it can be rich and insightful. Ask students to write about equivalence as well. Change the numbers (example: $\frac{3}{4} = 0.75$) to see if the concept is conserved!

Good Questions and Teacher Notes: Addition and Subtraction of Decimals

1. Write pairs of decimals to complete each column in the table.

Sums

Greater than 1	Equal to 1	Less than 1
0.76 + 0.44	0.55 + 0.45	0.2 + 0.35

Explain how you can tell whether the sum of two decimals will be *greater* than one. Explain how you can tell whether the sum of two decimals will be *less* than one. Explain how you can tell whether the sum of two decimals will be *equal* to one.

> Written as well as verbal explanations are much easier to give when students have examples from which to work.
>
> As students try to understand how decimals work, it is important to give them opportunities to formulate ideas of how decimal numbers operate. It is equally important for them to talk *and* write about these understandings.

2. Write pairs of decimals to complete each column in the table.

Differences

Greater than 1	Equal to 1	Less than 1
3.5 − 0.4	2.65 − 1.65	0.88 − 0.7

Explain how you can tell whether the difference of two decimals will be *greater* than one. Explain how you can tell whether the difference of two decimals will be *less* than one. Explain how you can tell whether the difference of two decimals will be *equal* to one.

> Comparing and contrasting the operations of addition and subtraction can provide meaningful instruction. Activities such as this also allow students opportunities to develop estimating strategies to approximate particular sums or differences.

3. Suppose you know the answer to Problem A. How can you use what you know about Problem A to solve Problem B? Solve both problems. Was your assumption correct?

PROBLEM A   PROBLEM B

72.15   72.15
−23.79   −43.79

> Too often students rely solely on computation to assess the reasonableness of an answer. The ability to estimate is powerful and useful. Estimating the magnitude of one answer by using information available from another can be an effective strategy.
> Offering students opportunities to predict results and to identify patterns of calculations is important. Try a similar approach with addition of decimals.

4. Write a story problem with an answer of 12.2. Your problem should require the addition of three numbers.

> Giving a context to a calculation can be difficult. It not only requires a degree of mastery with the procedure but also an understanding of how the numbers need to relate to one another.
> Much addition and even subtraction practice will result from such an activity as the students work to identify numbers that will adhere to the constraints of the given problem.

5. Work with the digit sets 1234 and 987. You may insert a decimal point just before, between, or after each given set of digits. You cannot change the order of the digits. You may add zeros only if they do not change the value of your number. Find ways to insert the decimal points so that you can get five different

sums using these two sets of digits. What is the largest sum that you can make? What is the smallest sum?

> Students can often generalize their understanding of addition with whole numbers to addition with decimal numbers. The requirement of manipulating the decimal points allows students the opportunity to make important generalizations about how, when, and where decimal points in numbers affect sums.

Good Questions and Teacher Notes: Multiplication and Division of Decimals

1. The mean of a set of four numbers is 5. Three of the numbers are 4.3, 8.15, and 1.65. What is the fourth number of the data set? How did you find it?

> Division as well as addition and estimation proficiency are required by such a question. You could ask follow-up questions such as: "What would you have to do to the data set to get a *higher* mean? A *lower* mean? How would the data set be different if you needed to add two numbers?"

2. Which of the following problems has the largest product? Try to figure it out by solving as few of the problems as possible.

3.2 × 17	50 × 3.5	1.7 × 50
24 × 2.9	2.4 × 29	5.0 × 36

> The ability to assess and estimate the magnitude of products will help students determine which numbers to try. Important calculation practice is often hidden when students are working to solve an intriguing problem.

3. Can you create a problem in which the product of two decimals is *smaller* than either of the numbers being multiplied? What was your strategy?

> Possible Solution: $0.14 \times 0.4 = 0.056$. When two numbers less than one are multiplied, the product will be smaller than both of the numbers.
>
> A great deal of multiplication practice will be carried out as students work to find decimal numbers that will adhere to the constraints of this problem.
>
> Finding one solution may not allow the students to make generalizations about their findings. It may be necessary to encourage students to find multiple solutions before they make conjectures.

Fractions, Decimals, and Percents

4. Can you create a problem in which the product of two decimals is *larger* than either of the numbers multiplied? What was your strategy?

> Possible Solution: $1.6 \times 1.7 = 2.72$. When two numbers greater than one are multiplied, the product will be greater than both of the numbers. If one of the numbers is less than one and the other is greater than one, the product will be larger than only *one* of the numbers.
>
> Understanding how multiplication affects the products of various types of decimal numbers allows students to make sense of the rules that govern multiplication computations. Such an understanding can enable students to make more accurate estimates and assess the reasonableness of computations.

5. Create a story problem with a quotient of 3.4. Solve your story problem. How did you go about choosing your numbers?

> Having students create story problems can give teachers a lens through which to view students' conceptual as well as procedural understandings. Being given the solution and then being asked to work backward can be a challenge for some. It is often the conceptual understanding, or lack of such, that can cause difficulties with a task like this. It requires careful reading on the teacher's part to assess the accuracy and appropriateness of a context.

> **H** Assign story problems requiring different constraints, operations, or even multiple operations.

Percents (Grades 5–6)

EXPERIENCES AT THIS LEVEL WILL HELP CHILDREN TO

- move comfortably between differing representations of rational numbers
- compare and order rational numbers
- use benchmarks that relate different forms of representations of rational numbers
- develop methods for solving problems involving rational numbers
- use estimation to help make decisions

MATERIALS

- hundredths grid (see Blackline Masters)
- calculators
- sale flyers from local newspaper

Good Questions and Teacher Notes

1. How can you

   change a percent to a fraction?
   change a percent to a decimal?
   change a decimal to a fraction?
   change a decimal to a percent?
   change a fraction to a decimal?
   change a fraction to a percent?

Give a numerical example and a written explanation for each situation, and use drawings when you can.

> It becomes increasingly important for students to be able to move flexibly among the representations of fractions, decimals, and percents. Using friendly-denominator fractions (factors of hundred) can help solidify concepts of equivalence as students move from one to the other.

2. Using hundredths grids, shade in the following amounts [see Blackline Masters]. Write equivalent representations using a fraction and a decimal.

   50%

   25%

   75%

   80%

> Using an area model can help students make sense of the multiple representations of the same quantity.

3. Place these fractions, decimals, and percents on the number line. Use a different number line for each set of numbers. Explain the reasoning of your placement of each number.

$$0----\tfrac{1}{2}----1----1\tfrac{1}{2}----2$$

25%, 1.55, $\frac{2}{3}$, 75%

$\frac{1}{4}$, 1.49, 88%, 45%

0.05, 0.5, 50%, 0.55

Order counts! This activity can serve students well if the follow-up is done as a class discussion. Such a forum can be used to push the clarity of students' thinking and language.

4. *California* has twelve letters.

What fraction of the state name is made up of vowels?
Write the above fraction as a decimal.
What percent of the state name is made up of consonants?
What fraction of the state name is made up of the letter *a*?
What percent of the state name is made up of the letter *c*?
Write the above percentage as a decimal.

Can you name a state of which more than 50 percent of its letters are vowels?

These conversions may not be so neat and tidy. Instruction on rounding can be more meaningful and useful when applied in a problem-solving context. Calculator usage may be an option once conceptual understanding of how conversions work is established.

Asking students to create their own state riddles and conversion questions can help support the thinking required to move flexibly between fractions, decimals, and percents.

5. Pure Hockey is having a sale of 30 percent off all shin guards. If CCM shin guards sell for $59.99, what is the amount of the discount? If Bauer shin guards sell for $44.99, what is their price after the discount? If I have $50 in my wallet, can I buy a pair of Bauer shin guards with a 5 percent sales tax? Show your thinking and calculations.

Discount problems are popular in most textbooks—and practical because of their real-life application. It is important, however, to ask a series of varied questions. What is the discount? What is the new price? How much more money will I need to make a purchase?

 Using sales flyers from newspapers can offer opportunities for continued meaningful application. Students can create their own percentage questions within constraints set by the teacher or class given the prices on a flyer.

6. Alissa and Linda conducted a survey of the students in their mathematics class. They found out the following information: 75 percent of the students in the class do homework three or more nights each week. Of the students who do homework three or more nights a week, half do homework five nights each

week. From the information given, can you tell how many students are in the class? Explain why or why not.

> Percentages represent *comparisons,* not exact quantities. Therefore, students *cannot* tell how many are in the class given the information presented. Ask students to present different possible answers. For example: If there are forty kids in the class, thirty kids do homework three or more nights. Of those thirty kids, fifteen do homework five nights a week.

Fractions (Grades 7–8)

EXPERIENCES AT THIS LEVEL WILL HELP STUDENTS TO

- interpret fractions as parts of wholes, parts of sets, locations on a number line, and as ratios
- order and compare fractions, decimals, percents, and integers
- translate fractions into decimals and percents
- recognize situations that call for the multiplication and division of rational numbers
- multiply and divide fractions
- interpret fraction multiplication and division computations
- estimate the products and quotients of fractions

MATERIALS

- pattern blocks
- calculators

Good Questions and Teacher Notes

1. I have a pile of pattern blocks. Two-thirds of the blocks are trapezoids. There are one-fourth as many triangles as trapezoids. The remaining shapes are hexagons. How many of each shape could there be in this pile?

> Put pattern blocks on students' desks so that students can answer this question concretely as well as abstractly. In the discussion of students' answers, ask students what their answers have in common. Why, for example, are the numbers of hexagons and triangles always the same? Also note that you could ask a similar question using decimals and percents.

2. Mark kept track of the number of times he scored a goal during one hockey practice and the number of attempts during one practice session. At the end of

the session, he said, "I made two and a half times as many shots as I missed." What fraction of Mark's attempts might have been goals?

> Mark is comparing one part of his data with another. In order to answer the question, students must translate from this part-to-part comparison to one that compares a part with the whole. One possible answer is that Mark made fifteen shots and missed six, so that fifteen–twenty-firsts or five-sevenths of his attempts were goals.

3. Find a fraction that is less than $\frac{2}{1,000}$ but greater than $\frac{1}{1,000}$.

> One way to answer this question is to translate the fractions into decimals, find a decimal number that is greater than 0.001 but less than 0.002, and write that decimal number as a fraction. This question can be modified by changing the denominator.

4. Louisa had to put a list of fractions, decimals, and percents in order from least to greatest. Her method was to translate all numbers into percents and put the percents in order from least to greatest. But she then forgot to write the numbers in their original forms. What might the original numbers have been?

62.5% < 75% < 80% < 160%

> The most obvious answer can be found by converting the percents to fractions with denominators that are powers of ten. By looking beyond this answer and investigating other equivalents, however, students will develop facility with common fraction-decimal-percent conversions.

5. Estimate the location of each point on the number line.

> Make sure that students refer to their answers as *signed numbers* and not integers.

6. Give the length and width of a rectangular room that has an area of $24\frac{1}{4}$ square yards.

> As students work, look to see whether they apply what they know about solving whole number area problems to find the length and width of the room.

7. The mixed numbers in the following problem are missing. Use the partial products to find the two mixed numbers.

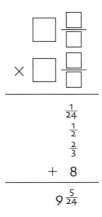

Help students make the connection between the partial-product method for multiplying two-digit whole numbers and the partial-product method for multiplying mixed numbers. Also, after students find different solutions to the problem, encourage them to find connections between them.

8. Eugenio estimated the answer to a fraction multiplication computation by finding half of a number close to eight. What might have been the computation?

Since Eugenio is using estimation, it is not necessary for one fraction to be exactly equal to one-half. Instead, this fraction can be close to one-half. For example, $\frac{4}{10} \times 8\frac{1}{9}$ is similar to taking half of a number close to eight.

9. Find two denominators that make the number sentence true. What conclusions can you make? [The common-denominator approach to solving division of fractions is one that many students can make sense of and apply successfully. For more information on this algorithm, see Van de Walle (1998).]

$$\frac{9}{?} \div \frac{2}{?} = 4\frac{1}{2}$$

Once students share their answers, they should come to the conclusion that the denominators must be the same for the number sentence to be true. Following this discovery, ask students to test their conclusion with another pair of numerators that have the same denominators.

10. Frank looked at a fraction division computation and said, "I know the answer will be a whole number." What might have been the computation? What do you think Frank noticed?

Fractions, Decimals, and Percents

One way to engage students in a discussion of this question is to make a list of students' answers and then ask them to make generalizations about the numbers in the computations. For example, if students generate the answers $\frac{1}{2} \div \frac{1}{4}$, $\frac{3}{5} \div \frac{1}{5}$, and $\frac{9}{2} \div \frac{3}{2}$, students may notice that the denominator of the dividend is always a factor of the denominator of the divisor and the numerator of the divisor is always a factor of the numerator of the dividend.

11. Piper looked at a fraction division computation and said, "I estimate that the answer will be close to sixteen since I can subtract the divisor from the dividend approximately sixteen times." What might the computation have been?

The repeated-subtraction interpretation of division helps students make sense of computations where the divisor is a fraction. One possible answer to this question could be $3\frac{9}{10} \div \frac{1}{4}$.

12. How can you solve $2\frac{1}{4} \div 14$ using a simple four-function calculator without pressing the decimal point key?

If necessary, clarify to students that a simple four-function calculator does not have a fraction key.

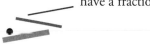

Decimals (Grades 7–8)

EXPERIENCES AT THIS LEVEL WILL HELP CHILDREN TO
▨ order and compare decimals with other representations of rational numbers and other types of numbers
▨ understand the relationships between terminating and nonterminating decimals
▨ convert decimals into fractions and percents and vice versa
▨ multiply and divide decimals
▨ estimate the products and quotients of decimals

MATERIALS
▨ base ten blocks
▨ calculators

Good Questions and Teacher Notes

1. Use base ten blocks to show a number that is greater than $3\frac{1}{5}$ but less than $3\frac{1}{4}$.

To answer this, students will have to assign values to the blocks that show decimal amounts less than one.

2. What would a Venn diagram of terminating, repeating, and nonterminating decimals look like?

Students may have difficulty differentiating between repeating and nonterminating, nonrepeating decimals. Contrasting the decimal equivalent of $\frac{1}{6}$ with numbers such as the square root of two and pi may help them make the distinction.

3. When you look at a fraction, how can you tell whether its decimal equivalent will terminate or not?

This is a very complex question that will likely require a lot of class time to discuss. One way to answer this question is to generate a list of fractions whose decimal equivalents terminate and look for a common feature. For more information on this topic, see *Math Matters* (Chapin and Johnson 2000).

4. A recent report published that 0.685 of the people in the town of Hanover participate in voluntary recycling. Write an attention-grabbing headline for this data.

The purpose of this question is for students to think about which form of a rational number is most appropriate for a given situation.

5. The volume of a rectangular shipping box is 4.125 cubic feet. What might the dimensions be?

One way students might solve this problem is to covert 4.125 to $4\frac{1}{8}$ and find three numbers with that product.

6. I multiplied two numbers and got a product smaller than both numbers. What numbers might I have multiplied?

Students can use calculators to help them answer this question. Asking students why the product is smaller will help students see that, as with fractions, multiplying decimals can be interpretted as taking part of a part.

7. A four-digit number was multiplied by a six-digit number to get a number close to two. What might these numbers have been?

By answering this question, students will learn that it is the relative size of decimal numbers and not simply their number of digits that is most helpful in estimating their product.

8. In the problem below, the decimal points were accidentally erased from the two numbers. Looking at the answer, what do you think the two numbers were?

$$
\begin{array}{r}
145 \\
\times\ 46 \\
\hline
870 \\
+\ 5800 \\
\hline
6.670
\end{array}
$$

> Trying to multiply every combination of decimal numbers is not an efficient way of answering this question. Instead, students should try to interpret the problem using what they know about multiplication and estimation.

9. Wanda looked at a decimal computation in her math book and said, "This problem is kind of like taking a third of a number that is close to one." Write a problem that fits this description. Solve your problem.

> Being able to interpret a decimal multiplication computation helps students solve the computation. It is of particular importance in judging the reasonableness of an answer.

10. I divided two numbers and got a quotient that was one hundred times greater than the dividend. What numbers might I have divided?

> After sharing students' answers, ask them why the quotient is greater than the dividend. If students seem confused by this question, prompt them to apply the repeated-subtraction interpretation of division to their computations.

11. How can you use a calculator to solve $0.2\overline{)4.58}$ without pressing the decimal point button?

> Answering this question will help students make sense of why we move the decimal point when the divisor is a decimal.

Percents (Grades 7–8)

EXPERIENCES AT THIS LEVEL WILL HELP CHILDREN TO
- interpret percents as comparisons to one hundred
- make sense of percents greater than one hundred

Good Questions for Math Teaching

- compare percents with other forms of rational numbers and other types of numbers
- solve problems about percent increase and decrease
- select appropriate operations when solving percent problems

MATERIALS
- optional: calculators

Good Questions and Teacher Notes

1. Use the digits 0, 1, 2, 3, 4, 5, 6, 7, 8, 9 exactly one time each to create numbers that fit this ordering: fraction < decimal < fraction < whole number < percent

> In order to answer this question correctly, students will need to create a percent greater than one, a concept they often struggle with.

2. The chance of rain, a sales discount, a likelihood of winning a carnival game, and the part of a dollar as written on a check were all equal but written in different ways. What might the different ways be? [NCTM 2000]

> Although there is an infinite set of fractions to choose from, students should choose ones that make sense in the given contexts.

3. A jewelry store is planning a "sale." It wants to offer 25 percent off its jewelry prices but have the customer pay just as much for the jewelry as if it were not on sale. How can this be done?

> Insist that students say more than, "The store increases its prices before the sale." Instead, require that students quantify such a statement by giving the percent of increase and justifying their answers with several examples.

4. Joan's parents bought her a basketball hoop for her birthday. As a result, her free-throw average has increased 110 percent. What might her average have been and what might it be now?

> Observing students explore percents greater than one hundred will give you keen insight into their understanding of percent as a *comparison* with one hundred instead of as a fraction out of one hundred.

5. A bag of jelly beans reads, "Now 33 percent more jelly beans in every bag!" How many jelly beans might have been in a bag and how many might be in a bag now?

Fractions, Decimals, and Percents

EXTENSION   You may wish to extend this question by asking students to bring in food labels that advertise similar percent increases.

6. Rachel moved to a new house in her town. Her bus ride is now 20 minutes shorter than it used to be. How long might Rachel's bus ride have been, and given this time, by what percent has her ride length decreased?

> Once students find the percent of decrease, ask them to describe Rachel's shortened bus ride using the phrase *times less than*.

7. Carla's average on four tests in math was 89.5 percent, but her percent score on each test was a whole number. What might have been Carla's test scores?

> One way to solve this problem is to find the product of 89.5 and 4. This would give the total of Carla's tests scores which can then be split into four different test scores.

8. Hoai calculated her test average after the first three tests of the school year. If she earns a 90 percent on tomorrow's math test, her average will increase to 85 percent. What scores might Hoai have earned on her first three tests?

> Students may answer that Hoai earned 80 percent on each of her first three tests. They may reason that this would result in a new average of 85 percent since the average of 80 percent and 90 percent is 85 percent. This answer is incorrect, however, because it does not give enough weight to her current average, which is based on three test scores.

9. A pollster found that exactly 36.$\overline{6}$ percent of people prefer two-door cars to four-door cars. How many people might have been surveyed?

> Do students know how to interpret tenths of percents? Do students think of using equivalent ratios to solve this problem?

10. If you pay 5 percent sales tax on three items, have you paid a total of 15 percent sales tax? Why or why not?

> This question will address a misconception that the percent of tax on each item should be added to find the total tax percentage. To help students see the flaw in this reasoning, ask, "So, if my test scores are twenty percent, forty percent, and thirty percent, does this mean my average is ninety percent?"

11. CDs are on sale at two stores. Fulton's sale advertises "Buy 1 get 1 free." Jordan's ad says "50 percent off all CDs." Where would you buy your CDs?

> Since percents are used so frequently in consumer affairs, instruction on percents should aim to make students more informed consumers.

12. Why do stores offer discounts such as 10 percent off when you open a credit card account?

> Since this question requires knowledge of credit card interest, you may wish to pose this question for homework so that students can discuss it with their parents. ■

8 Geometry

The study of geometry invites students to explore, describe, and compare lines, angles, and shapes. When we ask students questions based on these relationships, we are helping them prepare for the more formal study of geometry that will follow in later years.

Grades 5–6

EXPERIENCES AT THIS LEVEL WILL HELP CHILDREN TO

■ describe, measure, and predict angle measurements formed by intersecting lines with and without a protractor
■ explore sums of angle measurements of triangles and quadrilaterals
■ classify and compare properties of polygons

MATERIALS

■ rulers
■ protractors or angle rulers
■ blank paper
■ ∠HAT (see Blackline Masters)
■ colored paper
■ scissors/glue sticks
■ chart paper
■ clock faces (see Blackline Masters)
■ polygon sets (see Blackline Masters)
■ color tiles
■ straightedges
■ supply of paper: construction, specialty papers

Geometry has a language all its own. As children mature mathematically, it becomes increasingly important to use more formal geometric language. Keeping a visible word bank of geometric vocabulary is helpful as we encourage children to refine their talk about geometry.

Questions 1 through 3 require the use of a protractor. Protractor usage can be frustrating to upper-elementary-age students. The double scale of the traditional protractor can present difficulties as can figuring out where to put the protractor on the angle! Working through some of the angle vocabulary such as *acute, obtuse, right,* and *straight* will help students identify reasonable measures. If a student classifies an angle as acute and then finds a measure of 135 degrees, we all know something is amiss! A circle protractor can help with these issues, but practice is once again necessary in order for the students to determine where and how to set the protractor on the angle. The angle ruler that Connected Mathematics Project (CMP) promotes in its lessons is an interesting alternative. Not only can the students determine the measurement of an angle, but they can also see how open or closed the angle is by comparing the angle being measured with the angle ruler.

Good Questions and Teacher Notes

Questions 1 through 3 are based on this model:

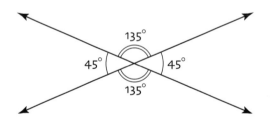

1. On a blank sheet of paper, construct two intersecting lines. Measure the four angles that the intersecting lines have created. What do you notice about the measures of the angles?

Construct another pair of intersecting lines. Measure the four angles that these lines have created. What do you notice about the measures of these angles? Can you make a generalization about intersecting lines and the measures of angles that they form?

Most students will notice that the *opposite (vertical)* angles are equal in measurement. It may be necessary to have the students repeat this exercise several times before they can make generalizations.

2. On a blank sheet of paper, construct two intersecting lines. Measure the four angles that the lines have created. What do you notice about the sum of two of the *adjacent* angles? What about the sum of the other two adjacent angles?

> Constructions and activities such as this allow students to develop understandings of fundamental geometric theorems. When two lines intersect, two adjacent angles form a straight angle, which measures 180 degrees. This activity can also support a discussion of *supplementary angles*.

3. On a blank sheet of paper, construct two intersecting lines. Measure the four angles that the lines have created. What do you notice about the sum of all four angles? Will this always be the case with any pair of intersecting lines? Why? Support your position with previous investigations [as in Questions 1 and 2] and understandings.

> Questions such as this lay the groundwork for developing the ability to make conjectures, which is integral to the study of formal geometry proof in years to come (Chapin and Johnson 2000, 160).

4.

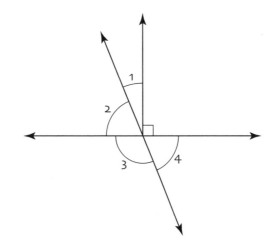

Without using a protractor, can you determine the measurements of the angles in this construction? Use what you know about vertical angles [they are equal], the sum of adjacent angles [180°], the measurement of right angles [90°], and the sum of the angles that meet at a *vertex* [360°] to determine angle measures.

> Students may be surprised at what they discover. They quickly make decisions about angle measurements based on what they already know is "true." Students also begin to realize the importance and benefit of reasoning and making conjectures based on informal geometric proof.

5.

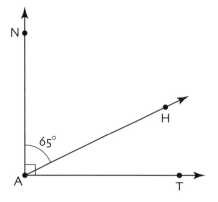

Given what you know about the measure of a right angle, what is the measure of ∠HAT? Support your position with what you know about angle measurement. If I told you that ∠NAH and ∠HAT were *complementary angles,* what could you tell me about measures of such angles? [See Blackline Masters.]

> The study of complementary angles (adjacent angles whose sum equals 90°) gives students another reasoning tool when studying angle measurement.

6. On a blank sheet of paper, construct a large *triangle* using a straightedge. Draw an arc in each angle. Cut out the triangle. Carefully tear off each angle. Reposition the angles so that they touch but do not overlap and glue them down on a piece of colored paper. [See example below.] What conjecture can you make about the sum of the angles of a triangle? Will this conjecture apply to all triangles? Try this activity with different triangles.

> Asking students to make conjectures that are based on self-discoveries and generalizations is necessary when we teach for understanding. Making posters of different triangles and the sums of their angles will tap students' creative energy as well as support their learning.

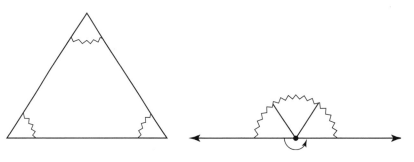

7. On a blank sheet of paper, construct a large *quadrilateral* using a straightedge. Draw an arc in each angle. Cut out the quadrilateral. Carefully tear off each

angle. Reposition the angles so that they touch but do not overlap and glue them on a piece of colored paper. [See example below.] What conjecture can you make about the sum of the angles of a quadrilateral? Will this conjecture apply to all classifications of quadrilaterals—in particular, regular and nonregular polygons? Try this activity with different quadrilaterals.

If following the investigation set up by Question 6, ask students to initially hypothesize about the sum of the measures of the angles of a quadrilateral. Do they think the sum of the angle measures will be greater than that of a triangle's? Or less? Why?

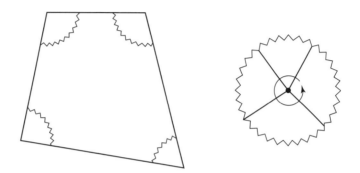

8. GUESS MY MEASURE

I am an obtuse angle.
All the digits in my angle measurement are odd.
None of my digits is the same.
The sum of my digits is thirteen.
All the three digits are factors of nine.
The digits are in ascending order.
What is my measure?

Although this may appear to be more of a number riddle than one of geometry, look again! Vocabulary becomes increasingly important as students solve and create geometry riddles. In this particular riddle, understanding the possible range of measures of an obtuse angle (>90° and <180°) is also important.

Having students create their own *Guess My Measure* riddles can help strengthen developing understandings about angle measurement and their use of geometric vocabulary. Creating a class word bank on chart paper of possible vocabulary words that could be used in various riddles can be helpful. Students will also find their knowledge of other mathematical topics helpful when creating clues.

9. At 12:00, the hour hand is pointed straight up at the 12. In each clock, mark where the minute hand is at the following times for the other side of an angle.

Sketch the angle formed by the hands on the clock and give the measure of the angle *without* a protractor. [See Blackline Masters.]

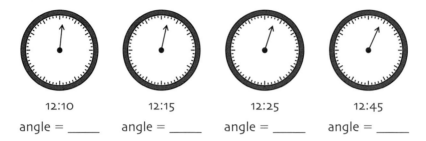

12:10	12:15	12:25	12:45
angle = _____	angle = _____	angle = _____	angle = _____

This activity will help students make the connection between the number of minutes in an hour and the number of degrees in a circle, a measure we adopted from the Babylonians.

Possible follow-up questions: What time creates an obtuse angle? An acute angle? A straight angle?

 What is so convenient about the number 360 when it comes to degrees?

10. How is each polygon the same in each set [see Blackline Masters]? Can you find a polygon that does *not* belong in each set? Can you find another polygon in the same set that might not belong for a different reason?

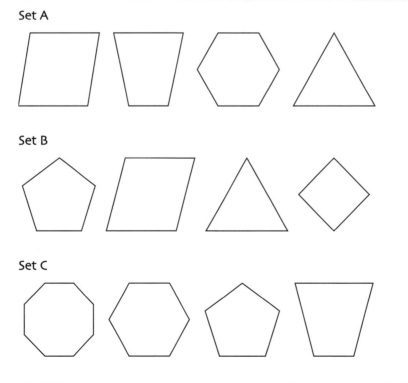

Set A

Set B

Set C

Good Questions for Math Teaching

Possible classifications:

SET A
■ No right angles.

SET B
■ All are regular polygons.

SET C
■ All the polygons have at least two obtuse angles.

Questions and investigations that ask students to identify and compare properties of polygons help develop higher levels of geometric thought. Finding properties that classify a set of polygons, as well as counterexamples within a set, can support the development of analytical reasoning skills and informal deductive thought.

Students could be asked to make their own sets and have other classmates determine grouping properties.

Questions 11, 12, and 13 address similar content but differ in their approach. Questions that present similar content can offer students additional opportunities to make connections between questions and the understandings they have acquired from solving them.

11. Philip has sketched a rectangle. The lengths of the sides of his rectangle add up to 26 inches. What could be the length and the width of Philip's rectangle? Use sketches to support your solution.

Some students may rely on their sketches (the use of color tiles also works well) to determine side length while others may prefer manipulating the numbers. Both methods will demonstrate a working understanding of the properties of rectangles.

12. Sketch and describe a polygon that can be made with the following side lengths: 5 inches, 5 inches, 8 inches, and 8 inches. Can you make other polygons with these same dimensions?

Parallelograms can be made, as well as a kite, depending on whether the equal sides are adjacent or opposite. The vocabulary that is necessary to describe solutions is rich and meaningful given the context of the problem and the properties of the sketched quadrilaterals.

13. Is this statement true or false: Any two quadrilaterals that have sides of same lengths will be identical in size and shape. For example, two quadrilaterals with

side lengths of 6 inches, 8 inches, 6 inches, and 8 inches will be the same size and shape. Give explanations and/or sketches to support your thinking.

> Although similar to Question 12, this question can also help fine-tune students' abilities to generalize their thinking and develop responses that will, over time, develop into more formal examples of geometric proof.

Two-Dimensional Shapes (Grades 7–8)

EXPERIENCES AT THIS LEVEL WILL HELP STUDENTS TO

- describe and compare angles that are formed by intersecting lines
- identify lines of symmetry, diagonals, and other characteristics of two-dimensional shapes
- use coordinate graphing to explore transformations (slides, flips, and turns) of geometric shapes
- determine if figures are congruent or similar
- explore the Pythagorean theorem

MATERIALS

- protractors
- graph paper (see Blackline Masters)
- rectangle ABCD (see Blackline Masters)
- photographs of people in different settings
- tangrams

Good Questions and Teacher Notes

1. Using your protractor, can you draw three adjacent angles that show at least one acute, one right, one obtuse, and one reflex angle? Name and measure each angle.

> One possible answer to this question is shown below.

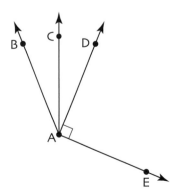

2. Create a Venn diagram that sorts examples of vertical, adjacent, and linear angles. What do you notice?

> By sorting examples of these three types of angles, students will come to realize that all linear angles are adjacent angles and that no adjacent angles are vertical angles.

3. A certain quadrilateral has diagonals that are not lines of symmetry. The quadrilateral has at least one line of symmetry. What might this quadrilateral look like?

> This question helps students focus on the difference between a diagonal and a line of symmetry. This question can be used as a launching pad into a full investigation of the diagonals of quadrilaterals. Classifying quadrilaterals according to their diagonals is a mathematically sophisticated and worthwhile task.

4. Find a quadrilateral that can be inscribed in a circle and one that cannot.

> For example, it is possible to inscribe only parallelograms that are also rectangles.

5. I can write each letter in the name *Ned* without picking up my pen or retracing any lines. For which other names is this true? For which names is it not true? Make a note of the patterns you see.

> Networks are an intriguing area of geometry with many real-world applications. For more information on networks, see *Mathematics: A Human Endeavor* (Jacobs 1970).

6. Describe a series of slides, flips, and turns that would move rectangle ABCD from Quadrant II to Quadrant I as shown below. [See Blackline Masters.]

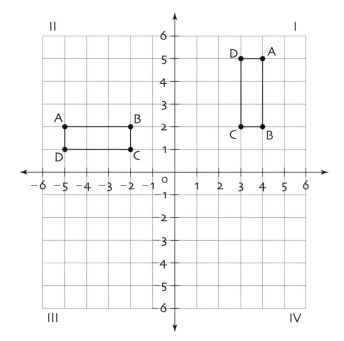

Students should specify the distances of translations, points and degrees of rotation, as well as orientations of reflections.

7. Draw a shape on a coordinate grid whose diagonals have slopes of $\frac{1}{2}$ and -2. [NCTM 2000]

The diagonals of each shape will be perpendicular.

8. We often hear the word *similar* in and out of school. Make a list of all the different situations in which you have heard the word used. How is the use of the word *similar* as used in math class related to its uses outside of math class? [Chapin, O'Connor, and Anderson 2003]

The various uses of the word *similar* (and many other words in the mathematical register) can cause confusion and lead to misconceptions for students. Discussing how a term varies in usage is crucial to a student's understanding of the concept associated with that term.

9. The coordinates of the vertices of triangle ABC are (2, 1), (4, 1), and (3, 4). Give the coordinates for the triangle DEF so that it is similar to triangle ABC. Identify the scale factor from triangle ABC to triangle DEF.

Students should use graph paper (see Blackline Masters) to help them think through this question. You can follow up this question with one that asks students to give the coordinates of two new similar triangles.

10. Police and surveillance companies use similarity to determine the height of robbers caught on videotape. How do they do this? [Lappan et al. 2002]

Students may need to look at photographs of people surrounded by familiar objects to successfully explore this question.

11. I drew a set of seven triangles. Five were similar to one another, three were congruent, and two were neither similar nor congruent to any other. What might these triangles have looked like? Draw the triangles and label their side lengths.

This question will help students understand that all congruent shapes are also similar.

12. Assigning a value of 1 to the side of the small square in the tangram set, use some pieces to create a figure that has a perimeter that is greater than 6 but less than 7 units.

Students should be comfortable using the Pythagorean theorem to answer this question since the numbers involved are small.

Three-Dimensional Shapes (Grades 7–8)

EXPERIENCES AT THIS LEVEL WILL HELP STUDENTS TO
- investigate properties of three-dimensional shapes
- create two-dimensional representations of three-dimensional shapes and vice versa
- explore transformations, reductions, and enlargements of three-dimensional objects

MATERIALS
- flat pattern shapes (see Blackline Masters)
- graph paper (see Blackline Masters)
- pictures or models of three-dimensional solids including cubes, rectangular prisms, cylinders, cones, and pyramids
- interlocking cubes

Good Questions and Teacher Notes

1. Make a case for why each one would not belong to the group: cube, rectangular prism, cylinder, cone.

This question, which can be repeated using different shapes, helps students see the similarities and differences between three-dimensional shapes.

2. Describe or draw a three-dimensional shape whose front, side, and top views are different.

If students are unfamiliar drawing views of three-dimensional shapes, they may need practice doing so before answering this question.

3. Using any number of the shapes below an unlimited number of times, make a flat pattern for a three-dimensional shape [see Blackline Masters].

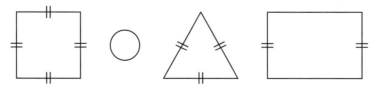

If you were to fold your flat pattern, what shape would it make?

You may need to help students name their shapes by letting them know that a prism and a pyramid are named by the shape of their base.

4. The faces of a cube are marked as shown below. Opposite faces have identical markings. Draw a flat pattern for this cube. [Musser and Burger 1988]

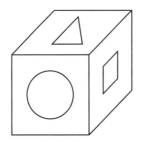

In order to answer this question, students will need to identify which squares on the flat pattern will become the opposite faces of the cube. Visualizing the transformation of a two-dimensional representation to a three-dimensional object is an important skill in the study of geometry.

5. Draw and label the dimensions of a flat pattern for a cylinder. Label the radius of the base and the length and width of the lateral surface.

Do students understand that the length of the lateral surface must be the same as the circumference of the base?

6. A standard six-sided die has six faces and is in the shape of a cube. Which other shapes can be used to make a fair die? Why?

Students may be familiar with other types of dice, such as octahedron dice and dodecahedron dice, but may not have considered why the geometric properties of these shapes lend themselves well to dice.

7. Find a three-dimensional shape with *at least one* axis of symmetry. How far can you turn the shape before it returns to its original position? [Van de Wall 1998]

An axis of symmetry is analogous to a line of symmetry of a two-dimensional shape. Introduce the term *order of symmetry* to describe the distance the shape is turned before it returns to its original position.

8. Describe a series of slides, flips, and turns that will result in the change in views of the shape shown below.

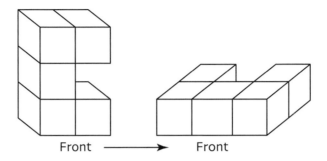

Front ——————▶ Front

Students may be familiar with transforming two-dimensional shapes but may never have applied the same ideas to three-dimensional shapes.

9. I have a rectangular prism made up of interlocking cubes. Eight cubes are totally hidden from view. How many cubes might be in the prism?

Students will develop their spatial reasoning skills by first answering this question without using the cubes and then checking their answer with the cubes.

9 Algebraic Thinking

Algebra is a vehicle for condensing large amounts of data into efficient mathematical statements (Chapin and Johnson 2000). When we ask students to think algebraically, we are asking them to formalize patterns, analyze change, understand functions, and move fluently between multiple representations of data sets.

Grades 5–6

EXPERIENCES AT THIS LEVEL WILL HELP CHILDREN TO
- understand equality
- understand the use of variables in different situations
- describe function rules using words and symbols
- identify, describe, continue, and generalize patterns
- represent patterns numerically, symbolically, and geometrically

MATERIALS
- Number Path A (see Blackline Masters)
- Number Path B (see Blackline Masters)
- color tiles
- graph paper (see Blackline Masters)
- patio borders (see Blackline Masters)
- pencil sharpener stories and graphs (see Blackline Masters)
- grouping patterns (see Blackline Masters)

The following questions have been created and adapted to develop and support *algebraic thinking* skills, not to promote a formal study of algebra in grades 5 and 6.

Students can be introduced to algebra as a way of thinking in the upper-elementary grades rather than as a formalized unit of study. When we ask students to predict, continue, and articulate patterns, functions, and generalizations, we are asking them to think algebraically. It becomes increasingly important for students to have an understanding of arithmetic procedures as they work to develop algebraic thinking skills. Both are extremely important as students describe mathematical relationships. Whereas arithmetic is effective in describing static pictures of the world, algebraic thinking skills allow students to describe and predict change and variation (Cuevas and Yeatts 2001).

The algebraic principles that these questions address are not necessarily discussed in the commentary following each question. The Lessons for Algebraic Thinking series, published by Math Solutions Publications, is an excellent resource for a discussion of the mathematics being addressed when working with students on algebraic thinking skills. Other resources are cited in the References.

Good Questions and Teacher Notes

1. The same shapes are the same numbers.

$$\square \times \square = 36$$
$$\square \times \triangle = 48$$
$$\triangle + \cap = 18$$
$$\square \times \triangle \times \cap = ?$$

What number does each symbol represent?

Sequences such as these can provide students with opportunities to push the flexibility of their thinking and operational understanding. Fractions can also be substituted for the knowns and unknowns.

 Given the same values listed above for $\square$, $\triangle$, and $\cap$, what is the value of $\diamond$? $[(3 \times \square) + (2 \times \triangle)] - \diamond = 2 \times \cap$

2. $168 \div a = b$

Find values for *a* and *b* that would make this number sentence *true*.
If $a = 12$, what is the value of *b*?
If the value of *a* increases, how will the value of *b* change?
If the value of *a* decreases, what happens to the value of *b*?

When we ask students to identify and generalize relationships, we are asking them to think algebraically. Many standard substitution questions can be extended to encourage children to identify patterns and operational relationships.

3. $\square + 0 = \square$ is a true sentence no matter what number is substituted for $\square$. Can you find other open number sentences that are true no matter what value is substituted for the unknown? Test your sentences by substituting values for the unknown(s).

> Questions such as this ask students to contemplate the existence of *identities*— open sentences that become true equations no matter what value is substituted for the unknown.
>
> Students may claim that $\square \div 0 = \square$. Take time to discuss why division by zero is not possible. It is not possible to "undo" or reverse this equation:
>
> $$\square \times 0 \neq \square$$
>
> Posting an ongoing list of found identities can be helpful for students as they discover mathematical properties such as the commutative property: $\square + \triangle = \triangle + \square$.

4. Match the "If" and "then" statements to make true sentences. Prove your selections.

If $n = 7$,	a. then $n^2 = 49$
If $n = 12$,	b. then $(2n + 3) \div 4 = 5$
If $n = 0$,	c. then $24 - (n + 6) = 6$
If $n = 8.5$,	d. then $(12 - n) \times \frac{1}{2} = 6$

> Computational practice is embedded in the solving and creation of "If . . . then" statements such as these. Other values of n and subsequent equations can be developed based on the computational skills being covered in class at the time.

5.
$$\begin{array}{r} a \\ + \, a \\ \hline c\,b \end{array}$$

What numbers can a, b, and c stand for? Can you find other solutions? What is always true about c? Why? What is always true about b? Why? [Greenes, Dacey, and Spungin 1999]

> Trial-and-error calculation will allow students the opportunity to generalize truths about the values of a, b, and c. Because there are multiple solutions, truths can be compared and contrasted in a class discussion.

6. A > B

   B > C

   C > D

   D > A

Can all of these statements be true? Explain why or why not. Can you insert another *relational* symbol to make this progression of statements true? Support your solutions with numerical proof.

> Algebra has a language of its own. Terminology should be used when the question presents a meaningful context for its usage. Understanding the difference between a *relational symbol* (one that designates a relationship between two quantities) and an *operational symbol* (one that designates an action, such as +, −, ×, or ÷) becomes increasingly important as students move toward more formal algebra instruction.
>
> Experimenting with other symbols and the substitution of numerical values will give students valuable thinking and articulation practice.

7. What is the *start* number? Justify your solution. [See Blackline Masters.]

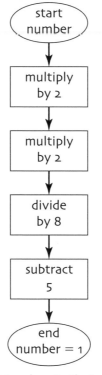

Number Path A

Undoing operations sets the stage for later work with simplifying equations.

 Have students create their own number paths making sure that they work both forward and backward.

8.

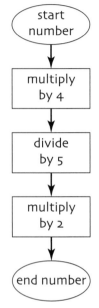

Number Path B

[See Blackline Masters.]

What is the end number when the start number is 5?
What is the start number when the end number is 16?
What is the start number when the end number is 40?
What do you know about the start number when you know the end number?
What do you know about the end number when you know the start number?

Looking for relationships between numbers and operations can help students predict and generalize patterns and/or outcomes.

 Choosing a start number that is a multiple of five will result in an end number that is a multiple of eight. Why do you think that happens?

Algebraic Thinking

9. Complete the chart. What is the rule? Write your rule in words *and* as an equation. Add three more pairs of In and Out values.

In	Out
5	8
10	13
3	6
0	?
?	45
?	?
?	?
?	?

Asking students to identify relationships between in the In column and the Out column is asking them to identify functions. For every In value, there is only one Out value, which is linked by a specific rule.

Often students will prefer to look for progressions *vertically*. Encourage students to also look *horizontally*. Not giving In values in numerical order pushes students to look at horizontal patterns.

Although the rule given in this particular chart may appear to be simple for some (+ 3), it presents a starting point that is accessible to all students. More complex rules can then be introduced as students become more comfortable and competent. When students make up their own sets of In and Out values, they seem to create increasingly complex rules naturally!

 Create a set of In and Out values for a classmate to solve.

10. Complete the chart. What is the rule? Add three more pairs of In and Out values.

In	Out
aardvark	a
giraffe	a
hippo	o
?	?
?	?
?	?

Even when using words, the Out value relies on a rule that links it to the In value. Starting with *aardvark* purposefully confuses students because the Out value for this particular set is the *second* vowel of the In value. Students begin to realize that it is often necessary to study several In and Out pairs before they can generalize a rule.

 Create a set of In and Out values *not* based on numerical values. You can use pictures, words, or designs. Be able to articulate your rule clearly.

11. Complete the chart. What is the rule? What would be the output value for any value (*n*)?

In	1	2	3	4	5	10	*n*
Out	4.5	7.5	10.5	13.5	?	?	?

Presenting another charting representation other than the traditional vertical T-chart can be helpful for students as they develop flexibility in their thinking.

 Create a set of In and Out values for a classmate to solve.

12. My bird feeder is set up for winter. On the first day, five finches come to my feeder. On the second day, six finches come to the same feeder. On the third day, seven finches arrive. Each day, the number of finches increases by one more than the number of finches that arrived at the feeder the day before. At this rate, how many finches will arrive at the feeder on the tenth day? Create a chart to identify the pattern. Explain the pattern in words.

The ability to create tables and/or T-charts (horizontally and vertically) to chart and extend patterns is a useful problem-solving tool. The ability to then articulate and symbolically represent those patterns is equally useful.

 On the first day, five finches come to my feeder. If the number of finches increases by four each day, how many finches will arrive at the feeder on the tenth day? Create another T-chart to continue the pattern. Explain the pattern in words.

13. What would come next in this sequence? 1, 4, 9, ___, ___, ___

Can you draw a picture to represent this growth? Can you write a rule in words and symbols to find the next term? Can you find another way to represent the growth of this pattern?

Algebraic Thinking

Because this pattern represents exponential growth, a question such as this could accompany a number theory unit. Each term can be represented by a square formation, which can help students identify the squareness of the numbers.

This sequence can also be represented graphically, which can help students see the nonlinear, nonconstant growth of the sequence.

 Follow the same procedure for this sequence: 1, 3, 6, ___, ____, ___.

14. Using color tiles, create a pattern of squares that fits this T-chart describing its growth.

Stage Number	Total of Squares
1	3
2	6
3	9
4	12
5	15

How is your pattern growing? Sketch your pattern. Describe your rule in words. Compare your pattern with a classmate's. What is the same about your patterns and growth? What is different? How many squares would there be in the tenth stage? How do you know? In the one hundredth? How many tiles would be in any stage (n stage)?

You should encourage students to describe predictable growth. When growth is predictable, students can see it by looking at what stays the same at each stage *and* at what changes.

The *Piles of Tiles* activity from *Lessons for Algebraic Thinking, Grades 3–5* (Wickett, Kharas, and Burns 2002, 197) presents various investigations such as this in greater detail and depth.

15. Imagine that the following pattern continues:

Row 1	3		
Row 2	3	6	
Row 3	3	6	9

Good Questions for Math Teaching

| Row 4 | 3 | 6 | 9 | 12 | |
| Row 5 | 3 | 6 | 9 | 12 | 15 |

.   .   .   .   .   .

.   .   .   .   .   .

What numbers will be in Row 6? What is the last number in Row 10? In which row is 45 the last number? Explain how to find the last number in a row. [Greenes and Findell 1998]

Looking at the row numbers and the last numbers can help students identify the pattern.

Row Number	1	2	3	4	any row
Last Number	3	6	9	12	row number $\times$ 3

Note that the In and Out (x and y) values in Questions 14 and 15 are representations of the same growth pattern.

16. The pattern continues. Fill in the blanks.

$$2 \times 4 + 1 = 3 \times 3$$
$$3 \times 5 + 1 = 4 \times 4$$
$$4 \times 6 + 1 = \_\_ \times \_\_$$
$$\_\_ \times 7 + 1 = \_\_ \times \_\_$$
$$\_\_ \times \_\_ + \_\_ = \_\_ \times \_\_$$

Describe patterns that you see. What will the equation look like when the first term is 25?

Asking students to identify and continue patterns within patterns helps develop their abilities to continue multiple patterns within a sequence.

Equality is also addressed in problems such as these because of the need to operate on both sides of the equation.

17. Look at the pattern in the figures below. If the pattern continues, how many white squares will be in the border of a patio with one hundred shaded squares? Explain how you know. Can you give a rule to determine how many squares will be in this border? [See Blackline Masters.]

Algebraic Thinking

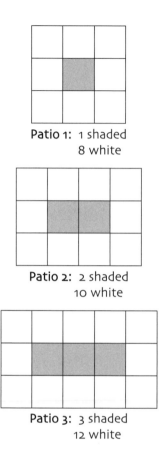

Patio 1: 1 shaded
8 white

Patio 2: 2 shaded
10 white

Patio 3: 3 shaded
12 white

Thinking algebraically requires students not only to determine what comes next in a pattern but also to generalize beyond a geometric representation.

A multicolumned T-chart can be used to organize the data for this problem.

Asking students to look at patterns both vertically and horizontally will help them generalize patterns and make predictions.

Patio Number	Number of Shaded Tiles	Number of Border (White) Tiles	Total Number of Tiles in Patio
1	1	8	9
2	2	10	12
.	.	.	.
.	.	.	.
.	.	.	.

18. Which graph matches which story? [See Blackline Masters.]

Good Questions for Math Teaching

You are working on a math investigation and you realize that your pencil needs to be sharpened . . .

Story A	You get up. Walk toward the pencil sharpener. Stop to answer a question at Molly's table. Walk on to the pencil sharpener. Sharpen your pencil. Walk back to your table.

Story B	You get up. Walk to the pencil sharpener. Sharpen pencil. Walk back. On the way back, you drop your pencil and break its point. Stop and laugh with Jeffrey. Pick up pencil. Walk back to the pencil sharpener to resharpen the pencil.

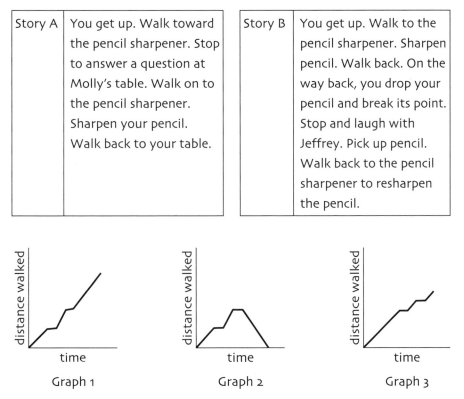

Graph 1   Graph 2   Graph 3

Graphic and symbolic representations of motion are common in the formal study of algebra. In answering this question, students are asked to compare *intervals of time* with *intervals of distance walked* as they fit stories to graphs. A conversation about the inappropriateness of Graph 2 for either story given its shape may be necessary.

19. This graph represents Lindsay's time and distance during a 10K run. How would you describe the course?

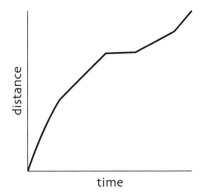

A graphic representation is a story about relationships between two values within a given context. If you give students one and ask them to create the other, you are offering students opportunities to construct understandings about such relationships.

20. Without graphing the points, determine which graph fits these ordered pairs. How can you tell?

(2, 3)

(2, 6)

(2, 4.5)

(2, 0)

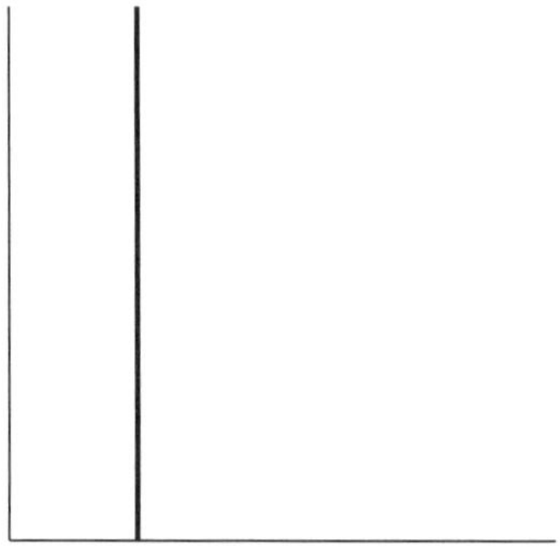

Graph A

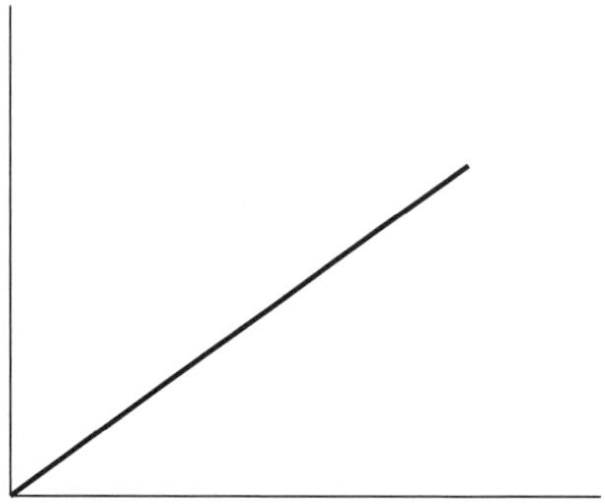

Graph B

Graph C

Asking students to assess and make generalizations about graphs as they identify change and constant values can support them as they learn to reason about graphic representations and relationships.

 Explain graphs in which the *y* values are the same. What could the graph look like? Create a situation or story in which these values would make sense.

21. What could be happening in these graphs? What could be changing (or not) as time goes by? Choose a graph and create a story that describes the change. [See Blackline Masters.]

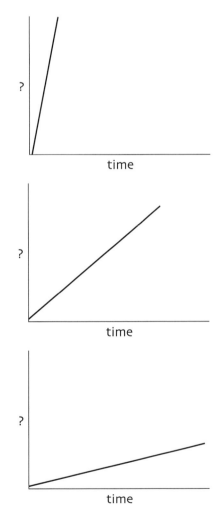

Looking at graph shapes without numbers on either axis allows students opportunities to make conjectures about the qualities of the shape of each graph, such as the steepness of the line *(slope)* and growth or change over time.

Algebraic Thinking

22. Write a number sentence that fits the picture of the groupings below [see Blackline Masters]. Are there other ways you can group the dots? Write a number model for each new grouping.

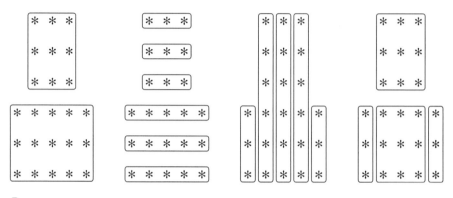

Responses:

$$15 + 9 = 24 \qquad 3(3) + 3(5) = 24 \qquad 2(3) + 3(6) = 24 \qquad 2(9) + 2(3) = 24$$

Because each picture has a total of twenty-four dots, equality can be demonstrated by comparing two number models, such as $15 + 9 = 2(3) + 3(6)$. It becomes increasingly important to challenge a common misconception that equates the equals sign with *the answer is* rather than a representation of balance and equivalence.

If creating number models to fit the picture is difficult for some students, ask them to match the number models to the pictures.

Grades 7–8

EXPERIENCES AT THIS LEVEL WILL HELP STUDENTS TO

- describe, create, and connect multiple representations of data sets
- express pattern rules both iteratively and explicitly
- discriminate between linear and nonlinear functions
- explore the different uses of variables
- understand the concepts of slope and *y*-intercept
- create equivalent algebraic expressions and linear equations
- solve simple linear equations using principles of equality and by undoing operations

MATERIALS

- toothpick shapes and tables (see Blackline Masters)
- walk-a-thon graphs (see Blackline Masters)
- graph paper (see Blackline Masters)
- candy scatter plot (see Blackline Masters)
- perimeter and area tables (see Blackline Masters)
- sunflower growth (see Blackline Masters)

Good Questions and Teacher Notes

1. The students in Mr. Borenstein's math class were playing *Guess My Rule*. Mr. Borenstein planned to show the students pairs of starting and final values and ask the students to use the information to determine the rule. Mr. Borenstein wrote the first pair in the extended T-chart as shown below. [Lawrence and Hennessy 2002]

Starting Value	Using the Rule	Final Value
4		12

What could the rule be? Do you know for sure?

> Once students realize that one pair of values is not enough information to determine a function rule, ask them to name an additional two pairs of values and a rule that works for all three pairs.

2. During a round of *Guess My Rule*, the students in Mr. Rossetto's class correctly identified the rule as "The final value is three less than twice the starting value." What three pairs of starting and final values could be placed in this table that would satisfy this rule? [Lawrence and Hennessy 2002]

Starting Value	Using the Rule	Final Value
	Final value = 3 less than twice the starting number	

> Ask this question once students have had many experiences determining the rule when given starting and final values. See *Lessons for Algebraic Thinking, Grades 6–8* (Lawrence and Hennessy 2002) for more information on *Guess My Rule*. You may wish to use the discussion of this question to introduce some important terms and relationships in the study of functions. For example, you

could explain to students that the starting values can also be called the *domain* of the function and the final values can be called the *range* of the function.

3. Mrs. Batista's class uses a coordinate graph to play *Guess My Rule.* The graph below shows several points that indicate pairs of starting and final values for the rule $y = x$, where x equals a starting value and y equals a final value. Identify a rule that would result in points that were steeper than the ones shown. How do you know? Identify a rule that would result in points that were less steep. How do you know?

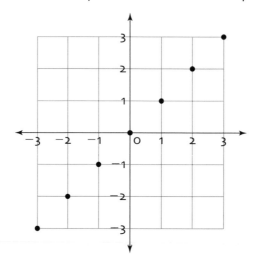

Developing a visual benchmark for $y = x$ and comparing it with other linear equations are important parts of developing algebraic reasoning.

4. Neila has been investigating the two patterns shown below. [See Blackline Masters.]

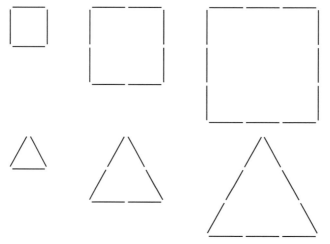

She made the charts below to show the relationship between the length of a side of the shape and the total number of toothpicks needed to make that shape. If Neila were to make a graph of the data in each chart, how would the graphs be similar? How would they be different?

Side Length	Number of Toothpicks	Side Length	Number of Toothpicks
1	4	1	1
2	8	2	6
3	12	3	9
10	40	10	30
n	$4 \times n$	n	$3 \times n$

Being able to analyze a chart with data about a pattern and use that information to describe a graph of the pattern is an important part of algebraic thinking. Make sure that in the discussion of this question, students address the differences in the rates of change in the two patterns and how they affect the look of each graph.

5. Nadia and Raphael plan to take part in a dance-a-thon. They will ask sponsors to donate money for each hour that they dance. They each made a chart that showed the relationship between money raised per sponsor and hours danced. They looked at their charts and made the following statements:

Nadia: The amount of money I will raise will be ten more than my time.

Raphael: The amount of money I will raise will be twice as much as my time.

What do these statements reveal about how Nadia and Raphael will earn their donations?

Students may need to actually make charts showing the changes in the amount of money raised for Nadia and Raphael in order to answer this question.

6. Two walkers in a walk-a-thon graphed their distance over time. They looked at their graphs and noticed that their lines were parallel. What does this reveal about the walkers? If they had made tables comparing distance to time, how would their tables be similar? How would they be different? [See Blackline Masters.]

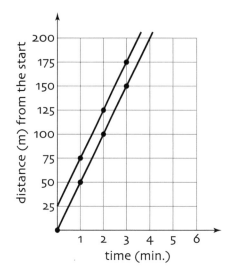

Since parallel lines have the same slope, the walkers have the same walking rates but different starting points. To help students understand this, ask them to make a chart of distance over time for each walker and compare and contrast the data.

7. Kevin just bought a car that cost $24,000. His car will depreciate in value 10 percent each year. Kevin made a graph to show the car's depreciation over time. What could the graph look like?

Students need experiences with graphs that have negative slopes. After students describe what the graph would look like, ask them to make a graph of the car's depreciation over time so that they can confirm or amend their descriptions.

EXTENSION   You may wish to extend this question by asking students to create a table that shows the car's depreciation over time as well as write a rule Kevin could use to find the value of his car at any given time.

8. Every year at Open House, the PTO hosts an estimation contest where a jar is filled with candy and whoever comes closest to guessing the total number of candies wins the candy. Lana really wants to win this year so she has been preparing at home. She has filled jars with candies, estimated how many candies are in the jars, and then found the actual amounts. Her data follows. What does this data reveal about Lana's estimating skills? How can this data help Lana win the contest? [See Blackline Masters.] [Lawrence and Hennessy 2002]

Good Questions for Math Teaching

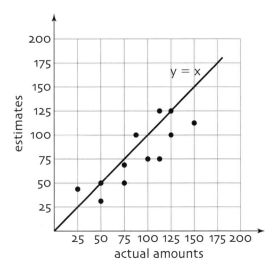

Focus the discussion on the meaning and relevance of the line $y = x$, the points above it, and the points below it.

9. Donna was studying for an upcoming math test. She looked back at her notes from a class on patterns made from pattern blocks. She found the following two statements:

Each stage has a constant of four blocks plus one block for each stage number. Each stage has one more block than the previous stage.

She wondered if it was possible that these two generalizations were describing the same pattern. What do you think? How do you know?

It is possible that the generalizations are describing the same pattern since the first is an explicit rule and the second is an iterative rule. One way for students to develop proficiency with explicit rules is to connect them with iterative rules for the same pattern.

10. Jair and Hermine were making growth patterns using square tiles in math class. Jair looked at one pattern and said, "I see a constant of two and then add the stage number."

Hermine said, "I see a constant of one and then add one more than the stage number." Is it possible that Jair and Hermine were looking at the same pattern? Why or why not?

Describing explicit rules for patterns is often a challenge for students in the middle grades. This challenge is further complicated by the fact that there are often many ways to describe a rule explicitly (Lawrence and Hennessy 2002). Talking

Algebraic Thinking

in math class about how explicit rules for the same pattern are alike can help students with this challenge.

11. Sabina earns money by baby-sitting. She offers her clients two different payment options and presents them in the graph below. What do you think each payment option is? How did you figure it out? [NCTM 2000]

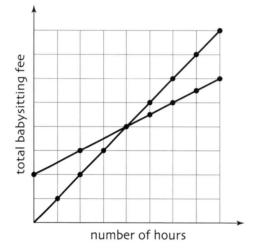

Once students explain what they think the options are, ask them why parents would choose either payment plan. The context of this question can be changed to other situations such as checking account balances, parking lot rates, and distance traveled over time.

12. The following sign is posted at the Clarence Library:

FINE POLICY FOR OVERDUE BOOKS
Twenty-five cents per day plus an additional $.50 for reshelving. Maximum fine of $5.

What might a table or graph look like that the library could also display to help people calculate their fines?

Have students post their tables and graphs. Then explore the relationships between the words, the chart, and the graph. For example, ask students how to use an entry in the chart to find a point on the graph and vice versa. Ask students how to use the wording of the policy to locate a specific point in the graph and vice versa.

13. Mario is investigating a problem about growing squares. The side length of the squares grows from 1 to 2 to 3 units, and so on. The perimeters and areas of

the squares change accordingly. Mario made a chart to show the relationship between the side length and the perimeter and another to show the relationship between the side length and the area. If Mario were to make a graph of each set of data, how would the graphs be similar? How would they be different? [See Blackline Masters.]

Side Length	Perimeter
1	4
2	8
3	12
10	40
n	$4n$

Side Length	Area
1	1
2	4
3	9
10	100
n	$n \times n$

Focus the discussion of this question on rates of change. Students should observe that both charts show growth, but one shows growth at a constant rate while the other does not. Spend time discussing how this difference in rate of change will affect the look of the graphs.

14. Three students took part in an after-school science club. Each student planted a sunflower and observed its growth over time. The graph below shows this data. Create a table that represents the x and y values of the graph. How has each student's sunflower changed over time? [See Blackline Masters.] [Meyer and Diopoulos 2002]

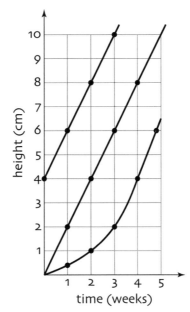

You may wish to incorporate the words *slope* and y-*intercept* in the discussion of this question. For example, you could ask, "What is the slope of each line? What does the slope tell us about the plants' growth?" Or "Why does only one line have a positive y-intercept? What does this tell us about that plant?"

15. What is the same and what is different about how the letter *m* has been used in the following three statements?

Alissa jumped 3 m.
$3 \times m = m \times 3$, for all numbers *m*.
If $3m + 2 = 14$, $m = 4$.

Because letters have so many different uses in mathematics, it is important not only to present students with mathematical statements that use letters in various ways but also to specifically discuss what role the letter plays in each situation.

16. Hamdi and Julie have two different cell phone plans. They want to compare them to see if one offers a better buy. They each made a graph showing the relationship between the number of calls and the total money owed. Hamdi said, "My graph has a greater slope than yours."
    Julie said, "My graph has a greater y-intercept than yours."
    What do these statements reveal about Hamdi's and Julie's cell phone plans? What might a sketch of their graphs look like?

Exploring their applications in real-life contexts gives meaning to the concepts of y-intercept and slope.

EXTENSION   Extend this question by asking if the line showing Hamdi's data will ever cross the line showing Julie's data and what this means about determining which plan offers the better buy.

17. Jean Pierre has just learned that the slope of a line is the ratio of rise to run and that in the equation $y = mx + b$, *m* represents the slope of the line. His teacher shows him this equation of a line, $y = 3x + 4$, and asks him to determine its slope. Jean Pierre thinks there must be some mistake since 3 is a whole number and not a ratio. Do you agree? Why or why not?

A whole number *m* expresses a ratio of some rise to a run of one. This happens when the change in *x* is a factor of the change in *y*.

EXTENSION   Extend this question by asking these two questions, which push for generalizations about slope: When is *m* a whole number? When is *m* a fraction?

18. Carla and Fiona are having a mathematical debate about the equation $y = \frac{1}{2}x + 3$. Carla thinks that every time y changes by one, x changes by two. Fiona thinks that every time y changes by one-half, x changes by one. What do you think?

> Students should use multiple representations to support their positions including graphing the equations and making a table of values. They may also decide to use what they know about equivalent and complex fractions to support their positions.

19. Maura is organizing a school fair. She is in charge of hiring vendors, choosing games and activities, and deciding on prices for admission, activities, and food. During a planning meeting with the fair committee, Maura wrote the equation $y = 2x + 5$. What might it be referring to?

> This question encourages students to think creatively about how linear equations are used in real-life situations. One possible answer is as follows: There is a $5 entry fee and each game or activity costs $2. So, the equation would show the total amount of money each person would spend at the fair on admission and games.

20. For homework last night, Jorge had to simplify four expressions. He wrote his answers without copying the original expressions. What might they have been?

 a. $10x + 3$
 b. $\frac{1}{2}x$
 c. $\sqrt{a - b}$
 d. $^-3a - 6$

> This question focuses on combining like terms. Look for the common misconceptions in students' answers:
>
> a. $10x + 3 = 12 - 2x + 3$
> b. $\frac{1}{2}x = \frac{1}{2} + x$
> c. $\sqrt{a - b} = \sqrt{a} - \sqrt{b}$
> d. $^-3a - 6 = ^-3(a - 2)$

21. Sal explained how he solved a linear equation by saying, "I undid the addition by subtracting from both sides. Then I undid the multiplication by dividing both

sides. That told me the value of x was ten." What equation might Sal have solved?

> Undoing, or reversing, operations is an effective way of solving linear equations and upholds the idea of an equation as a balance.

22. Tara and Tom were solving linear equations. To find the value of x in a linear equation, Tara asked herself, "What number, when you subtract four from it, is equal to twelve?" Tom solved a linear equation by adding four to both sides. Is it possible that the two students were solving the same equation? How do you know?

> It is possible that the students were solving the same equation. For example, the equation could be $x - 4 = 12$. It is important not only to use different methods for solving linear equations but then to compare and contrast them.

23. The hand shown is covering a term in a linear equation. What might the hidden term be and what, as a result, would be the value of x?

> You may need to remind students that a term is a number, variable, or the quotient or product of a number and a variable.

10 Data Analysis and Probability

In middle school, students are asked not only to collect and display data but also to discuss, analyze, and understand the correspondence among data sets and their graphic representations (NCTM 2000). Questions that ask students to reflect on notions of chance will help them better understand and apply basic concepts of probability to their daily lives.

Data Analysis (Grades 5–6)

EXPERIENCES AT THIS LEVEL WILL HELP CHILDREN TO

- develop strategies for collecting, representing, comparing, and reporting data
- analyze data sets according to statistical landmarks such as mean, median, mode, range, and sample size

MATERIALS

- chart paper
- graph paper (see Blackline Masters)
- mystery line plots (see Blackline Masters)
- investment graphs (see Blackline Masters)

Some of the following questions require the making of charts and/or graphs that will represent data about a particular class. It will be necessary to post chart paper with directions about the particular data collection before students answer the questions.

Good Questions and Teacher Notes

1. [On a large sheet of chart paper, make a Venn diagram. Label the circles *I love fractions* and *I love mystery novels* or any other classifications that you think would be interesting to your students. Have students place their names in the Venn where they belong, reminding students to place their names on the outside of the Venn if they fit neither category.]

What does it mean if someone is placed outside of the two circles? What does it mean if someone is placed in the intersection? Write three statements about your classmates from the data displayed on the Venn diagram.

> As students grow in mathematical maturity and sophistication, it becomes equally important for them to be able to express their opinions and observations with greater clarity. Posing a simple question such as "What do you notice?" offers opportunities for students to refine their wording and written conclusions.

2. The sixth grade is planning a movie night in the theater. Molly is conducting a survey about movie interests of the sixth graders in order to gather information for possible movie choices. If Molly asks her classmates one categorical question and one numerical question, what could the questions be?

> A question such as this asks students to think about the *kinds of responses* a data set can generate, not necessarily the data set itself.

3. [Post the following question on the board or on a piece of chart paper: What is your favorite field game (e.g., soccer, baseball, SPUD, etc.)? Have this data available for the students as they answer the following questions.]

Organize this data into a line plot. What is the mode of the data? Who would be interested in this data? What would the data tell them? Does your data have a mean? Why or why not?

> Students can be easily confused as they try to articulate the difference(s) between numerical and categorical data. Although this data can be graphed and analyzed, it is *categorical*, which makes finding a mean impossible.

4. Make a data set representing the ages of students with the following statistical landmarks:

Sample size: 12 students
Range: 8 years

Median age: 12.5 years
Mode: 10 years

Will everyone's data set look the same? Why or why not?

> Creating their own data sets requires students to have greater understanding of the identified statistical landmarks.
>
> Working backward, as students are being asked to do in this question, can be difficult for some. Sharing possible data sets as a class will help those who find this type of thinking difficult.

5. The mean number of children in six families is four. How many children might be in each family? Can you make a line plot to represent this data?

> Some students may approach this as a factors-and-multiples problem. Others may create a line plot first and adjust the data as they fit the plot to the constraints of the problem. The approach students take in answering this question may prove to be more enlightening than the answers they come up with.

6. Adam and Lauren have just bought a pet rabbit. The owner of the pet store told them that the median lifespan of a rabbit is seven years. What could a data set for the lifespan of twenty-five rabbits look like?

> Given the information in the question, students may assume that *every* rabbit will have a median age of seven, *every* rabbit will live to be only fourteen years old, and/or the highest piece of data *must* be fourteen. Discussions about outliers, sample size, and even the general health of those rabbits in the data set can set up convincing arguments in support of any of the positions.
>
> A question such as this can also lead students to the realization that data does not always help us make informed choices.

7. Each plot shows a different set of data about a sixth-grade class. Match the plots with the given data sets and justify your choices. [Everyday Learning Corporation 2002]

```
                        X
              X   X   X
              X   X   X   X       X       X
      X               X   X   X   X   X   X   X       X       X       X
  ─────────────────────────────────────────────────────────────────────────
  52  53  54  55  56  57  58  59  60  61  62  63  64  65  66  67  68  69  70  71
```
Plot 1

```
                                          X
                  X           X   X               X       X
      X               X       X       X   X           X       X       X   X   X
  ─────────────────────────────────────────────────────────────────────────
  48  50  52  54  56  58  60  62  64  66  68  70  72  74  76  78  80  82
```
Plot 2

```
          X
  X       X
  X       X       X
  X       X       X
  X       X       X       X       X       X       X
  ───────────────────────────────────────────────
  0       1       2       3       4       5       6
```
Plot 3

```
                          X
                  X   X       X       X
      X       X       X   X   X   X       X       X       X
  ─────────────────────────────────────────────────────────
  26  28  30  32  34  36  38  40  42  44  46  48  50  52  54
```
Plot 4

```
                                  X
              X                   X               X       X
  X               X       X       X       X       X       X               X
  ───────────────────────────────────────────────────────────────────────
  0       1       2       3       4       5       6       7       8       9       10
```
Plot 5

DATA SETS	PLOT NUMBER
A. Number of hours watched of TV last night	_____
B. Ages of younger brothers and sisters	_____
C. Heights, in inches, of some sixth graders	_____
D. Ages of some sixth graders' grandmothers	_____

Explain how you selected the line plot for Data Set D.

Explain why you think the other line plots are not correct for Data Set D.

What data set could represent Plot 4? Explain your thinking.

What other answers did you consider for each set of data? How did you exclude data sets for each line plot?

> Identifying what is likely versus what is unlikely will help students match the data sets with the line plots. The range and distribution of the data will help students make judgments and conclusions.

8. Mrs. Jacobs gave a math unit test worth 100 points. Following the test, she organized the scores into a stem-and-leaf plot. State five conclusions Mrs. Jacobs could make about her students' performance. Make reference to vocabulary words such as *range, median, mean, mode,* and *sample size* in your conclusions. What do you think the unit of study was? Why?

0	5
1	
2	4
3	4 9
4	3 7
5	7 9
6	1 6 8
7	3 5 5 6 8
8	3 6 6 6 7
9	2 5 6

> Stem-and-leaf plots offer students opportunities to identify clusters and patterns in a data set rather than focus on individual data items. Stem-and-leaf plots are also helpful when data covers a large range.
>
> Giving students opportunities to discuss and apply chosen representations of numerical data (e.g., line plot, bar graph, stem-and-leaf plot) will help them better assess appropriate and useful representations.

9. Which of these two graphs would you choose to convince potential consumers to invest in your company? Why? [See Blackline Masters.] [Chapin and Johnson 2000]

Increase in Sales per Month

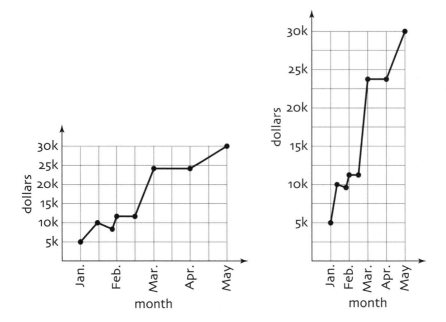

Both graphs display the same data. Because the intervals on the *x* and *y* axes are different on the two graphs, one *appears* to show more rapid growth. Graphs can be deceiving and improperly scaled to prove to consumers what producers want to prove!

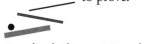

Probability (Grades 5–6)

EXPERIENCES AT THIS LEVEL WILL HELP CHILDREN TO

- understand that some events involve chance
- understand the concepts of likely and unlikely, fair and not fair
- develop strategies for reporting and interpreting both experimental and theoretical probability
- understand that probabilities are useful for making decisions

MATERIALS

- dart board (see Blackline Masters)
- bags of marbles (see Blackline Masters)
- blank spinner faces (see Blackline Masters)
- colored pencils

The study of probability can cut across all strands of mathematics. The applied arithmetic required by probability activities is rich and varied. Probability questions can and should accompany many units of study. Introduce a day of probability study as a diversion from the everyday occurrences of math class, designating it as "Probably Monday" or whichever day it is.

1. The probability of a particular event happening is $\frac{2}{5}$. Explain the probability of the event not happening. What could the event be?

A number line can be a helpful visual aid to support students' thinking about the relative certainty of an event happening.

		50%		
0		$\frac{1}{2}$		1
impossible	less likely		more likely	certain

Asking students to identify the probability of an event *not* happening can be counterintuitive. As we help students develop probabilistic thinking skills, we need to offer them opportunities to identify and/or differentiate between events that will *always* happen, those that will *sometimes* happen, and those that will *never* happen.

2. Assign Regions A, B, C, and D to this dartboard [see Blackline Masters] on which the probability of landing on Region A is $\frac{5}{8}$. If Courtney threw sixty-three darts, how many might land in Region A? Explain your reasoning. How can your understanding of fractions help you with this task?

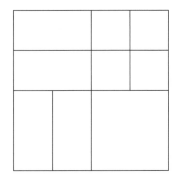

Although students may intuitively realize that they are manipulating fractional parts when answering this question, we need to offer students opportunities to explicitly make those connections between concepts and procedures.

Data Analysis and Probability

3. To play this game at a math carnival, a player picks one marble from each bag. Bag 1 contains equal amounts of red, blue, and yellow marbles. Bag 2 contains equal amounts of red and blue marbles. [See Blackline Masters.] If the colors of the marbles match, the player wins a prize.

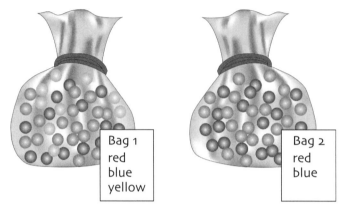

Bag 1
red
blue
yellow

Bag 2
red
blue

What are the possible outcomes of the game? What are the chances that a player will win a prize? Is this a fair game? If not, how could you change the rules or the game so that it would be a fair game? Explain your thinking. What are the possible outcomes of your new game in support of your adjustment(s)?

Charting outcomes is a valuable mathematical tool. Tree diagrams, matrices, and pictures can all be useful representations.

It's important to determine the purpose of this question before you pose it. Will this question be used as an opportunity to teach charting techniques? Or can you assume that your students have a level of proficiency with techniques of charting, which will then allow them to focus on the fairness of the game?

4. Describe how you could make a spinner that had four equally likely outcomes. What fraction of the circle would each section be? Make a drawing of your spinner using colored pencils. Can you think of another way to divide the spinner? Make a drawing of that spinner as well. [See Blackline Masters.]

Students may quickly divide the spinner into four equal adjacent parts. Asking them to come up with another way to divide the spinner will give students the opportunity to apply what they already know about fractions. Dividing up a spinner into eight equal regions with two each of the same color—but not adjacent to each other—may generate some interest. If time allows, have students test out their different arrangements.

5. Design a spinner with five spaces so that the chance of landing in one space is twice the chance of landing in each of the other four spaces. Give the

degree measurements of each central angle. [See Blackline Masters.] [Lappan et al. 2002]

Probability questions such as this not only assess an understanding of how likely an event is to happen but also offer students opportunities to practice computational skills.

6. Suppose that out of one hundred spins, you land on red eighty-two times and you land on blue eighteen times. What might your spinner look like? Color in your spinner. Explain your reasoning. How confident are you in your decision? [See Blackline Masters.]

Some students may color 82 percent of the spinner red and 18 percent blue whereas some may color 75 percent red and 25 percent blue, saying that not enough spins were made to determine exact percentages. The more spins, the closer the spins will come to the actual percentages or the theoretical probability of the action.

 Suppose out of 300 spins, you land on red 222 times and land on blue 78 times. What does your spinner look like now? How does this spinner differ from your last spinner? How confident are you in your decision now?

7. Sarah has designed a spinner with red, blue, yellow, and green sections. The chance of landing on red is 50 percent, the chance of landing on blue is 30 percent, and the chance of landing on yellow or green is 10 percent each. Suppose you spun Sarah's spinner 50 times. How many times would you expect to spin red? Blue? Yellow? Green? What if you spun it 100 times? How about 150 times? Explain your thinking.

It is helpful to let students make conjectures and to support those conjectures with an understanding of probable outcomes. Look for thinking that demonstrates an understanding that spinning more times can move the experimental probability closer to the theoretical.

EXTENSION   Asking about possible outcomes after 225 spins will stretch those students who are ready for a challenge.

8. Imagine that you have three colors of marbles in a bag: red, yellow, and blue. Imagine that you could pick out one marble without looking. The probability of picking a red marble is $\frac{1}{2}$. The probability of picking a yellow marble is $\frac{1}{3}$. And the probability of picking a blue marble is $\frac{1}{6}$. How many marbles of each color could be in the bag? How do you know? What could a picture of your answer look like?

There are many possible entry points when answering this question. Some students may actually want to try the experiment. Having bags and red, yellow, and blue marbles available (or colored chips, linking cubes, or crayons) may be necessary for some children. Drawings may help. Some students may move straight to paper-and-pencil calculations and the use of common denominators:

$$\frac{1}{2} + \frac{1}{3} + \frac{1}{6} = 1$$
$$\frac{3}{6} + \frac{2}{6} + \frac{1}{6} = 1$$

At the very least, there would be three red marbles, two yellow marbles, and one blue marble.

> **H** Pose a similar question with different fractions of marbles that add up to one. For example: there are four different colors of marbles in a bag: red, green, yellow, and blue. The probability of pulling out a red or a blue marble is $\frac{1}{4}$. The probability of pulling out a green marble is $\frac{1}{3}$. The probability of pulling out a yellow marble is $\frac{1}{6}$. What is the fewest number of marbles of each color that could be in the bag? How do you know?

9. Red Sox player Johnny Damon has tried to steal second base thirty-two times so far this season. He has been successful twenty times. Do you think his chances of stealing second base the next time he tries are good or bad? Explain your reasoning. Can you base your decisions solely on the numbers, or could there be other circumstances that might affect Damon's percentage of stolen bases?

Making assumptions based on approximations can be useful. Knowing that Damon steals successfully more than 50 percent of the time is often enough to start a conversation about his success rate.

Interesting conversations may be initiated by your baseball aficionados that may be based on opinions about the significance of the pitcher or an infielder. In this case, the numbers may not tell the whole story when it comes to statistics, probability . . . and baseball!

Data Analysis (Grades 7–8)

EXPERIENCES AT THIS LEVEL WILL HELP CHILDREN TO

- write questions, design studies, and gather data about a characteristic of a population
- use data taken about a sample to make conclusions about the population from which the sample was taken

■ choose, create, and apply appropriate graphical representations of data sets including histograms, stem-and-leaf plots, box-and-whisker plots, and scatter plots

■ interpret and compare data using measures of central tendency

MATERIALS

■ optional: calculators

Good Questions and Teacher Notes

1. Imagine you wanted to find out the favorite movie of students in your school. How would you accomplish this? What are the advantages and disadvantages to your plan?

This question presents a good opportunity to discuss different types of sampling, such as random sampling, convenience sampling, and voluntary response sampling.

2. A local newspaper reporter wrote an article claiming that more than 75 percent of the town's citizens thought the library fines were too high. Many readers wrote to the editor refuting the report, claiming that the sample for the survey was biased. How might the sample have been biased?

Helping students develop the ability to look beyond the headlines and evaluate their validity is an important skill in today's data-driven world.

3. You read in an ad: "Four hundred more people prefer the new and improved Bright Smile toothpaste to another brand." How might this data be misleading? [Lappan et al. 2002]

Students should consider the size of the sample as well as the way the survey was conducted (e.g., to what other toothpaste was the new and improved Bright Smile compared?) when answering this question.

4. Dana asked twenty-five of her classmates, "How many hours a night do you spend on homework?" She organized all of the responses into the box-and-whisker plot below. What might have been the twenty-five responses?

| 0 | 1 | 1.5 | 2 | 2.5 | 3 | 3.5 | 4 | 4.5 | 5 |

Data Analysis and Probability

A box-and-whisker plot marks the minimum value (excluding outliers), lower quartile (median of the data below the median), the median, the upper quartile (the median of the data above the median), and the maximum value (excluding outliers). Students should answer this question after they have had experiences interpreting and constructing box-and-whisker plots. Possible follow-up questions include:

> What could Dana say about half her classmates based on this data?

> What could she say about the number of students who do between 1.5 and 4 hours of homework?

5. Recently, two members of the student government surveyed the seventh-grade class and obtained the following results. What might their survey question have been?

Once students determine a sensible survey question, ask them to interpret the results using what they know about box-and-whisker plots. For example, a student might think that the survey question was "How many pets do you own?" That student should then be able to say, "Approximately half of those surveyed own two or more pets."

6. Ian's ice-cream shop opens at 11:00 A.M. and closes at 7:00 P.M. One day, Ian kept track of the number of customers in his shop each hour and recorded the information in a histogram. He noticed that the range of customers was twenty, and, on average, the number of customers in the store each hour was twelve. What might the histogram look like?

> Note whether students construct the histogram correctly. Specifically, since each bar in a histogram represents an interval, the bars should be drawn without spaces separating them. Students will need to decide whether to use the mean, median, or mode as the average.

7. Jean was interested in determining the frequency of *squares* (people whose arm spans and heights are equal) and *rectangles* (people whose arm spans and heights are different) in her class. She collected data on the heights (in inches) and arm spans (in inches) of everyone in her class and made a double stem-and-leaf plot to show her data. She concluded that six people are squares. Do you agree?

Height in Inches		Arm Span in Inches
999887776	5	36667778888999
533221110000	6	0000112

Students should realize that Jean's conclusion is faulty since the double stem-and-leaf plot separated the arm length and height for each person. A good follow-up question could ask students to consider graphs that *would* help Jean determine the number of squares and rectangles in her class.

8. Last year, I surveyed my students, asking them how long they studied for an exam. Then I made a scatter plot showing the relationship between hours spent studying for an exam and the exam results. What do you think this scatter plot looked like?

Helping students visualize a graph that shows certain conclusions can help them make sense of the features and purposes of such a graph. A good follow-up question to this one could be, "Why was a scatter plot a good choice for this data?"

9. In Mrs. Marvel's class, a student's grade is determined by the average of his or her seven test scores each term. At a recent parent-teacher conference, the following exchange occurred:

Mrs. Marvel said, "Tim's average is a C. And I have the data to show it."
Tim said, "I have an A average. And I have proof."
Tim's parents said, "Looking at your test scores, it looks to us like your average is a B." How could all three have proof of three different grades?

This question focuses on the discrepancies between the three measures of central tendency (mean, median, and mode). Spend time having students share their data sets of seven test scores that show the three different averages.

10. A recent survey asked a group of schoolchildren to rate, on a scale of 1 to 3, how much they enjoyed the school lunches. The average rating was 2.2. How many students might have been surveyed and what might their individual ratings have been?

One of the most prevalent real-life applications of decimals is data reporting. So it is important for students to learn how to interpret data reported with decimals.

Probability (Grades 7–8)

EXPERIENCES AT THIS LEVEL WILL HELP CHILDREN TO

- use tree diagrams, area models, organized lists, and knowledge of fractions to reason about chance
- find and analyze probabilities of independent and dependent events
- calculate probabilities of events when drawing with and without replacement
- use experimental probabilities to reason about theoretical probabilities and vice versa
- find the expected value of an outcome

MATERIALS

- optional: calculators
- dice of two different colors
- number tiles
- color tiles
- blank spinner faces (see Blackline Masters)

Good Questions and Teacher Notes

1. A cafeteria serves a lunch each day that consists of one appetizer, one entrée, and one dessert. The selections are made randomly from a limited number of items that does not change all year. Carla figured out that the probability of getting her favorite meal (carrot sticks, tuna fish on rye, and chocolate pudding) was $\frac{1}{24}$. How many appetizers, entrées, and desserts might the cafeteria choose from each day?

> While some students may be able to answer this question using the fundamental counting principle, others may need to make a sample menu.

2. Ryan thinks that the chance of rolling a sum of 4 with two dice is the same as rolling a sum of 5 because he thinks there are two ways to roll a 4 [(1, 3) and (2, 2)] and two ways to roll a 5 [(1, 4) and (2, 3)]. Do you agree or disagree? Why?

There are actually four ways to roll a five, (1, 4), (4, 1), (2, 3), and (3, 2), and three ways to roll a four, (1, 3), (3, 1), and (2, 2). Students often think that rolling (1, 4) is the same as rolling (4, 1) and count these two possible ways as one way. In the discussion of this question, have two different colors of dice available for students to use to help them make the distinction between different ways to reach a particular outcome.

3. Pete wants to play a game at a carnival where he'll open one of several boxes. Inside one of these boxes are some envelopes. Inside one of these envelopes is a hundred-dollar bill. Pete figured out correctly that he has a $\frac{1}{12}$ chance of winning. How many boxes and how many envelopes might there be?

> Encourage students to use an organizational tool, such as a tree diagram or an area model, to answer this question.

4. Maddie is playing a board game in which she rolls two dice, adds the numbers rolled, and moves that number of spaces on the board. Maddie can win the game on her next move if she rolls any one of three sums. She figures out that her probability of winning is $\frac{1}{4}$. What sums do you think Maddie needs to roll?

> Ask this question only after students have analyzed the likelihood of all possible outcomes of rolling two dice.

5. Jamie's favorite radio station is hosting a contest. At 8:00 A.M. tomorrow, the first fifteen callers will qualify for a chance to win a free trip to Hawaii. Only one of the fifteen callers will win the trip and the winner will be chosen randomly. Jamie figures she has a $\frac{1}{15}$ chance of winning the trip. Do you agree? Why or why not?

> Jamie needs to first consider the probability of being one of the first fifteen callers, which could be quite slim. Her chance of winning the trip is *dependent* upon her chance of being one of the fifteen callers.

6. A bag is filled with number tiles marked from 0 to 9. If you reach into the bag twice, with replacement, the chance of picking a 1 and then a 2 is $\frac{1}{4}$. How many number tiles marked 1 and 2 might be in the bag? What might be the total number of tiles?

> EXTENSION   Once students find an answer to this question, you may wish to extend it by asking what the probability would be if the tiles were drawn without replacement.

7. Tessa pulled color tiles from a bag and found that the experimental probability of drawing two red tiles without replacement was 35 percent. How many red tiles might have been in the bag? What might the total number of tiles have been?

> Since the given probability is experimental, a variety of answers is possible. For example, there may have been four red tiles and six tiles total, which would result in a $\frac{4}{6} \times \frac{3}{5} = \frac{12}{30} = 40$ percent chance of picking red, without replacement, which is close to 35 percent.

8. A weather reporter predicts that there is approximately a 40 percent chance of having rain on both days of the weekend. What might be the chance of rain *each* day?

> Weather reports rely heavily on probability. Therefore, instruction on probability should help students make sense of what they hear and read in these reports. One way to answer this question is to use an area model.

Rain on Saturday (80%)

Rain on Sunday (50%)

9. Austin was playing a game with a spinner. He figured out that if he spun the spinner one hundred times, about thirty-eight of the spins would land on the region(s) marked with an A. What might this spinner have looked like? [See Blackline Masters.]

> This question requires students to create a representation that matches a given probability. One way to answer this question is to recognize that $\frac{38}{100}$ is close to $\frac{37.5}{100}$, which is equal to $\frac{3}{8}$. So approximately $\frac{3}{8}$ of the spinner should be marked with an A.

10. A spinner is divided into red, blue, and green sections. Kevin expects for every three spins that land on red, two will land on blue, and there will be approximately three times as many red spins as green. What might this spinner look like? [See Blackline Masters.]

Help students connect the comparative language in this question with the probabilities of spinning each color. For example, since there will be three times as many red spins as green, the probability of spinning red must be three times the probability of spinning green.

11. Ruby spun a spinner that was divided into different-colored sections. After spinning one hundred times, she calculated that, experimentally, the probability of *not* spinning blue was 35 percent. What might this spinner look like? [See Blackline Masters.]

If no students show a spinner with several noncontiguous blue sections (that together add up to approximately 65 percent of the spinner), show one like this yourself.

12. The makers of Marla's favorite candy bar are having a contest. There is a coupon for a free candy bar hidden inside some candy bars. The candy bars cost $.60 each. Marla reads the probability of winning on the package and figures out that she would probably need to spend about $10 in order to win a free candy bar. What do you think is the chance of winning a free candy bar?

After sharing students' answers to this question, discuss whether or not this is a fair contest.

13. Leah and Sam were playing a game with two dice. They took turns rolling the dice and finding the products of the numbers rolled. To make the game fair, if Leah rolls a certain product she gets 2 points. If Sam rolls a certain product, he gets 3 points. What might the products be?

The inverse relationship between probability and payoff points is challenging for many students. For example, the probability of rolling Leah's product must be 1.5 times *greater* than that of rolling Sam's number since she gets 1.5 times *fewer* points than Sam.

14. Jorge was thinking about playing a game at his town fair. He calculated his probability of winning the $5 prize and found that if he plays ten times, he can expect to profit $10. How much might the game cost to play? What might be the probability of winning this game?

One possibility is a cost of $1 and a four-in-ten chance of winning: Jorge would spend $10 playing the game and win four times for a profit of $10.

Data Analysis and Probability

11 Measurement

In order to help students understand measurement, it is important to ask questions that will require them to both measure and make connections between the many relationships within measurement systems. Many measurement questions can be asked in conjunction with the study of other mathematical strands. We can use measurement to explore geometry, to collect and analyze data, and to develop proportional reasoning skills. The base ten conversions inherent to the metric system can also lend themselves well to the study of place value and decimal fractions. In the United States, the task of choosing appropriate measurement units is complicated by the use of both the customary and the metric systems of measurement. Whenever possible, students should be given the opportunity to develop familiarity with both systems.

Temperature, Time, and Length (Grades 5–6)

EXPERIENCES AT THIS LEVEL WILL HELP CHILDREN TO
- understand the importance of standard units
- estimate, make, and use measurements
- compute with and convert within customary units of measure

MATERIALS
- chart paper
- graph paper (see Blackline Masters)

Good Questions and Teacher Notes

1. Fill in the blanks with numbers. Make sure that the numbers apply to the context of the story!

> It was a beautiful June day. The temperature was _____°C at 7:30 A.M. Two and a half hours later, at _____, the temperature was _____ degrees warmer, or _____°C. Three and a half hours later, at _____, the temperature had risen to 30°C.

> A variety of procedures can be used to answer this question, such as guess-and-check or working backward from 30°C. The sense made by the chosen numbers is what matters most.

2. On March 4 at 10 A.M., the temperature in Boston was 33°F. The temperature rose *and* fell throughout the day. At 5 P.M., the temperature had fallen to 27°F. What might the temperature have been at each hour?

> Interpreting the positive or negative change on a thermometer can help students identify changes in temperature as well as give them a vertical number line reference.

3. [Ask students to post their bedtimes and waketimes for school days and nights on chart paper as they come into class. Then ask the following questions.]

   What is the range of sleep hours? What is the median number of hours of sleep for our class on a school night? What is the mean number of hours? What is the mode? What is the typical number of hours of sleep that your classmates are getting a night? Is this more or less than you thought it would be?

> Asking students to define what is typical for a data set pushes them to analyze and categorize data. Some may focus on the mode. Some may focus on the median. Some may focus on the distribution of data.

4. I am a measure of time.
   You can measure the length of a math class with me.
   There are sixty of me in an hour.
   I am equal to 60 seconds.
   Guess my unit.

> Asking students to devise their own *Guess My Unit* riddles with four or five clues will support students as they make connections between units of measure and identify attributes of their chosen measures.

5. What is your arm span in

> millimeters?
> centimeters?
> decimeters?
> meters?

If you find one measurement, how can you find the others without measuring?

> Greater understanding (and appreciation!) of the ease of metric conversions between units will develop when students are asked to measure with different units as well as to calculate one unit from another.

6. Fill in the blanks with numbers so that each story makes sense.

> Molly is making a batch of sugar 'n' spice cookies for her math class. Her recipe will make _____ dozen, or _____ cookies. The recipe calls for _____ c. of molasses and _____ c. of flour among other ingredients. Molly is to bake the cookies for _____ in a _____° oven.

> Jacob wonders what happened to his little chocolate lab puppy! When he first brought her home, Coffee weighed _____ lbs. Jacob fed Coffee _____ c. of puppy food each day. By the time Coffee was _____ months old, she weighed _____ lbs., _____ lbs. more than when Jacob brought her home! Jacob is worried. A full-grown lab can weigh as much as _____ lbs. Sometime soon, someone needs to tell Coffee that she can no longer be a lapdog!

> Filling in the blanks with the appropriate numbers helps students focus not only on the measurements but on their proper use within a context.

Weight (Grades 5–6)

EXPERIENCES AT THIS LEVEL WILL HELP CHILDREN TO
- understand the importance of standard units
- estimate, make, and use measurements
- compute and compare weight measurements and conversions

MATERIALS
- drawing paper and supplies (markers, colored pencils, crayons)
- weights (see Blackline Masters)
- dry rice and beans
- measuring cups
- scale

Good Questions and Teacher Notes

1. Make lists or pictures of things that weigh

   a. less than 1 kg
   b. between 1 kg and 5 kg
   c. between 5 and 20 kg
   d. between 20 and 50 kg
   e. more than 50 kg

   > Personal references or benchmarks can help make the process of estimation more accessible for students. U.S. customary measurements can easily be substituted.

2. Are these claims reasonable? Justify your position.

   a. My math teacher weighs 2,400 ounces.
   b. My math teacher drinks 70 ounces of water a day.

   > Both claims are reasonable. If an adult weighs 150 pounds, he should drink 50 percent of his body weight *in ounces*, according to many weight and conditioning coaches.
   >
   > Questions such as this give students the opportunity to develop a meaning for *ounce* given a context of weight or volume.

3. You want 5 pounds of weights. You have the following weights. Choose the fewest number of weights that totals 5 pounds. List the weights and numbers of each. Keep a record of your thinking. [See Blackline Masters.]

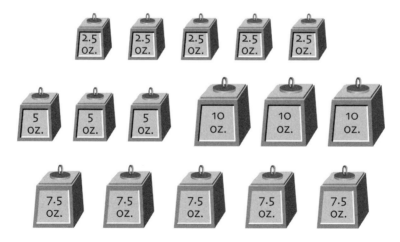

> Students are given the opportunity to practice calculation as well as conversion skills.

4. Rufus Mayflower, the toothpaste millionaire [Merrill 1999], knows that 500 lbs. is a quarter of a ton. Decide which of the following equations best represents how Rufus could have determined this. How do you know? Why did Rufus use the number 2,000? Why did he use the number 4? Could Rufus have figured out how many pounds are in a quarter of a ton any other way?

    a. $2,000 \times 4 = n$
    b. $2,000 \div n = 25$
    c. $2,000 \div 4 = n$
    d. $2,000 \times n = 4$

> Problem-solving strategies are employed when choosing the best representation. Asking students to explain why the other representations are not appropriate can be helpful when processing answers. Other quantities can be used to create similar questions, such as cups and gallons or ounces and pounds.

5. Many cooks around the world consider this expression to be a reasonable estimate: A pint's a pound the world around. What does this expression mean?

> One pint equals 2 cups. The rule implies that 1 cup of a food item weighs about $\frac{1}{2}$ pound, or 8 ounces.

6. [If possible, have a cup of dry rice and dry beans and a scale available for quick measures. Have students round their measures to the nearest ounce.] One cup of uncooked rice weighs about _____ ounces. [Fill in appropriate amount.] Knowing this, answer the following questions:

One pint of rice weighs about _____ ounces.
One quart of rice weighs about _____ ounces.
One gallon of rice weighs about _____ ounces.
One gallon of rice weighs about _____ pounds.

Would 1 cup of dry beans equal 1 cup of dry rice in capacity? In weight? Explain your thinking. Does the expression in Question 5 hold true?

> This question may help students make a distinction between capacity and weight. A cup is a measure of capacity. A pound is a measure of weight.

Area and Perimeter (Grades 5–6)

EXPERIENCES AT THIS LEVEL WILL HELP CHILDREN TO
- understand the importance of standard units
- estimate, make, and use measurements
- compute and compare areas and perimeters of plane figures

MATERIALS

■ color tiles
■ drawing paper
■ irregular polygon (see Blackline Masters)
■ cutout polygon models (see Blackline Masters)
■ scissors and tape or glue
■ graph paper (see Blackline Masters)

Good Questions and Teacher Notes

1. Describe two situations in which you want to know the *perimeter* of something. Units for perimeter are linear: cm, km, in., ft. Why?

2. Describe two situations in which you would want to know the *area* of something. Units for area are square units: cm², km², in.², ft.² Why?

3. Describe two situations in which you would want to know the *surface area* of something. Units for surface area are units²: cm², km², in.², ft.² Why?

> Identifying uses of these measures can help students apply understandings of area, perimeter, and surface area to real-life situations.
>
> As students begin to make the connection between the measurement label (whether linear or units²) and the actual measurement, they will be able to make better sense of procedures used to calculate perimeter, area, and surface area.

4. What could be the dimensions of a rectangle with 20 square units and whole number side lengths that has

    a. the largest perimeter?
    b. the smallest perimeter?

Explain how you found your answers for both a and b.

Can you make a generalization about shapes that will give you large perimeters?

Can you make a generalization about shapes that will give you small perimeters?

Would these same generalizations work with a rectangle of 100 units²?

Can you think of a real-life situation when the magnitude of the perimeter would matter?

"Skinny" rectangles will give the largest perimeter, which can easily be demonstrated with color tiles. Because the tiles will touch only on one or two edges, many edges are exposed.

If you are bordering a pool or a garden and only have so much money to spend on tiling or edging, then the perimeter measurement would have an impact on the shape of the pool or the garden.

5. What could the dimensions be of a rectangle with a perimeter of 16 units and whole number side lengths that has

    a. the largest area?
    b. the smallest area?

Explain how you found your answers for both a and b.

    Can you make a generalization about shapes with large areas?

    Can you make a generalization about shapes with small areas?

    Can you think of a real-life situation when the magnitude of the area would matter?

    Would these same generalizations about shapes work with a rectangle that has a perimeter of 100 units?

The rectangle that is most like a square will have the greatest area. Having students build the rectangles with color tiles will help them see the relationship between the shape of the rectangle and the area.

Giving a context to the answer will give greater meaning to the solution. Building a dog pen could be a context in which the area matters.

6. Molly says her rectangle has a perimeter of 30 units and an area of 50 units². Courtney says her rectangle also has a perimeter of 30 units but an area of 56 units². Can they both be correct? Explain. Use drawings to support your thinking. Can you think of a real-life situation when the dimensions of the rectangle would be important?

Many times students are convinced that shapes with a given perimeter have the same area. Encourage students to build or draw their shapes as they try to convince each other that Molly's rectangle can be 10 units by 5 units and Courtney's rectangle can be 7 units by 8 units. Giving a context to the answer will give greater meaning to the solution.

7. Kirsten says, "My rectangle has a greater area than yours."

    Scott replies, "My rectangle has a greater perimeter than yours."

    What might the dimensions of each of their rectangles be?

> Encourage students to draw and label their rectangles. Some students may be convinced that shapes with a larger area will have a larger perimeter as well.

8. Use *two* methods to find the area of this figure. Explain both of your methods. Is one more efficient than the other? Why or why not? [See Blackline Masters.]

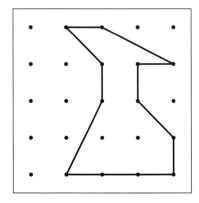

> Asking students to compute the area of irregular shapes helps extend their understanding of area and its calculation. Students will begin to realize that area can be constructed in many ways. Although the perimeter may change as the result of the reconfiguration, the area remains constant.

9. Can you always determine the perimeter of a figure if you know its area? Can you determine the area of a figure if you know its perimeter? Are area and perimeter related? If so, how?

> Displaying counterexamples (examples that disprove a yes response to either question) can help students see that knowing one measure does not necessarily mean you can determine the other.
>
>   Although area and perimeter are not directly related, they do tend to put constraints on each other.

10. A rectangle has the same area as a triangle whose area is $24\frac{1}{2}$ square inches. What might the dimensions of the rectangle and the triangle be?

> Embedding calculation work with fractions within the context of this question offers additional computational practice. Sharing strategies as a class will offer insights into the flexibility of students' manipulation of area computations.

Good Questions for Math Teaching

11. A rectangle has a perimeter of $18\frac{3}{4}$ inches. What might be the side lengths of a triangle with the same perimeter?

> When identifying side lengths of a triangle, it is important for students to consider that the sum of any two sides of a triangle must be greater than the third.

12. Can you fit a circle with a radius of 2.25 in. inside a circle with a diameter of 5.25 in.? Explain your thinking.

> Students may set about to calculate the areas of the two circles, when, in fact, area measurements are not necessary for answering this question. The relationship between the radius measurement and that of the diameter can help set up an initial response. The relative sizes of the circles can then be addressed.

13. You have been asked to help change the pricing of pizzas at Pepper Roni's Pizza Parlor. You can price pizza in one of three ways:

Suggestion 1: The price of pizza could be based on its diameter.
Suggestion 2: The price of pizza could be based on its area.
Suggestion 3: The price of pizza could be based on its circumference.

If you were to decide, which suggestion would you adopt? Explain. Give examples of your reasoning.

> Students may wish to calculate the diameter, area, and circumference of a specific-sized pizza before they generalize opinions. Remind students that their decisions need to be based on financial proof!

14. The circumference of each of Jonathan's bicycle wheels is 50 inches. How many rotations will Jonathan's wheels make in 1 mile? Explain how you calculated your answer. When would this information matter to Jonathan?

> Although conversion activities offer students opportunities to practice calculating skills, conversion charts and calculators may help students focus on the process of conversion rather than just on the calculation.

15. What happens to the area of a square when its dimensions are doubled? Tripled? Does the same pattern hold true for a rectangle? How about a triangle? Use cutout models [see Blackline Masters] to represent your reasoning. Create a chart to record your measurements.

> Be prepared for many misconceptions as students work to answer this question! Students will likely assume that doubling the dimensions can be equated to

doubling the area, when in fact the new area is four times greater! The same misconceptions may occur when students think about tripling the dimensions.

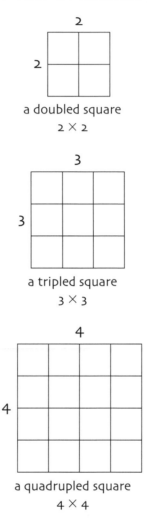

a doubled square
2 × 2

a tripled square
3 × 3

a quadrupled square
4 × 4

 What happens to the area of a square when you quadruple the dimensions? Does the same hold true for a rectangle? How about a triangle? Can you generalize a rule to predict the area of a square, rectangle, or triangle when its dimensions are increased any number (*n*) of times?

Volume (Grades 5–6)

EXPERIENCES AT THIS LEVEL WILL HELP CHILDREN TO

■ understand the importance of standard units

- estimate, make, and use measurements
- compute and compare the volume of three-dimensional shapes

MATERIALS
- volume pattern (see Blackline Masters)
- linking or Unifix cubes
- prisms (see Blackline Masters)
- graph paper (see Blackline Masters)

Good Questions and Teacher Notes

1. Describe two situations in which you would want to know the *volume* of something. Units for volume are units³—cm³, in.³ Why? How does this compare with what you know about perimeter and area measures?

> Volume is a measure of the amount of space occupied by a three-dimensional object. As students begin to make the connection between the measurement label (units³) and actual measurement, they will be able to make better sense of procedures used to calculate volume.

2. The pattern continues. What will be the volume of Figure 4? Figure 10? Figure 100? Explain your thinking. Can you create a rule to determine the volume of any figure that follows this pattern? [See Blackline Masters.]

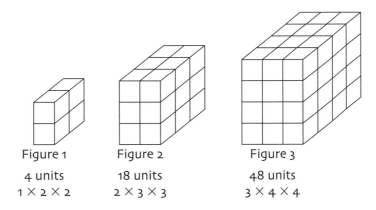

Figure 1	Figure 2	Figure 3
4 units	18 units	48 units
1 × 2 × 2	2 × 3 × 3	3 × 4 × 4

Having students build the prisms with linking cubes will help them see the pattern of growth. Encourage partner talk as the students build the prisms.

Students may find it helpful to chart the growth of the prisms. If they choose to do so, it is important that they can identify each number and what it represents and where it is on the prism.

Asking students to predict the volume of Figures 10 and 100 will help them develop the ability to generalize a rule from a pattern.

3. Estimate the length, width, and height of the following objects. Chart your estimations. What unit of measure will you use for each estimate? Check your estimates against another classmate's. What range of measurement would you consider to be accurate? What would be a reasonable margin of error?

   a. your desk/table
   b. a filing cabinet
   c. a dictionary
   d. a whiteboard/chalkboard eraser
   e. your classroom

> Determining an acceptable margin of error can lead to many interesting class discussions. Measurement is approximate by its nature. Students may determine that being off by an inch is OK for one item but not OK for another.

4. Adam uses ten blocks to build a four-step staircase. How many blocks will he need for a twelve-step staircase? How do you know? Create a number model to represent your answer.

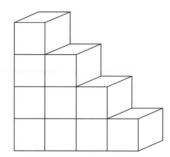

> Some students may need to build staircases to help them predict the number of blocks in a twelve-step staircase. Others may use the four-step staircase and extrapolate the numbers from that diagram alone.

5. Select the number set that indicates the most likely dimensions of each prism. The volume is given. [See Blackline Masters.]

   a. 4, 6, 10
   b. 2, 10, 10
   c. 5, 5, 5
   d. 3, 3, 9
   e. 3, 5, 9
   f. 5, 2, 15
   g. 2, 5, 8

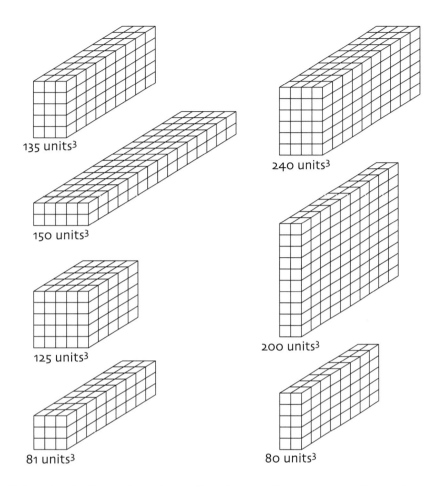

135 units³

150 units³

240 units³

125 units³

200 units³

81 units³

80 units³

Although calculating the volume of the lettered dimensions could result in correct matching, determining what measurements could *not* be matched with a specific figure using reasoning and logical thinking can also be employed. For example, c cannot be matched to 150 units³ because all of the dimensions of c are the same. The figure with a volume of 150 units³ does not have any dimensions of equal length.

6. A packaging factory wants you to build a box that will hold twice as many cubes as the box pictured below:

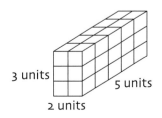

3 units

5 units

2 units

What could the dimensions of the new box be? How do you know? Draw your new box to scale using graph paper.

Students are asked to double the volume, *not* to double the dimensions. Some students may not realize that there is a difference between these two ideas.

EXTENSION   What happens to the volume of the original box when the *dimensions* are doubled? Is the volume of this box the same as the doubled volume of the original box?

EXTENSION   What would happen to the dimensions of the box if it needed to hold four times as many cubes? Eight times as many cubes? Can you identify a pattern? What also happens to the surface area as the volumes of all the boxes increase?

Creating T-charts will help students to chart the progressions of the volume as well as the surface area. Charting the growth will also help students to identify patterns and to make generalizations.

Weight (Grades 7-8)

EXPERIENCES AT THIS LEVEL WILL HELP STUDENTS TO

- weigh and estimate weights of common objects
- convert within and between systems of measurement
- choose appropriate units of weight for particular objects
- use known weights to estimate unknown weights
- relate weight to other attributes of objects (such as volume and area)

MATERIALS

- items weighing 1 gram, 1 kilogram, and 1 pound
- balance scales and spring scales
- flour
- measuring cups
- popped and unpopped popcorn
- rolled coins

Good Questions and Teacher Notes

1. Which unit(s) of measure would be most appropriate to measure the weight of each of the following items:

    a. a pillow
    b. a puppy
    c. a textbook
    d. a sofa

Good Questions for Math Teaching

The ability to determine a suitable unit of measurement is a very important measurement skill.

2. Think of objects whose weights you would measure in each of the following units.

    a. grams
    b. kilograms
    c. pounds
    d. tons

> To help students answer this question, have items available that weigh 1 gram, 1 kilogram, and 1 pound. Also, you may wish to tell students that 1 ton equals 2,000 pounds. Students can use the weights of these items to estimate the weights of others.

3. I went shopping and found a 1-pound box of Snowflake Sugar Cubes for $1.70. A 1-kilogram box of White Cloud Sugar Cubes offered a better buy. How much might the White Cloud Sugar Cubes have cost?

> Give students the conversion (1 pound = 0.454 kilogram) so that they can estimate a possible price. Students should realize that 1 pound is about the same as half of 1 kilogram.

4. Identify two objects where one weighs less but has greater volume than the other.

> Introduce the term *density* when discussing this question.

5. A medium-size cat weighs 6 kilograms. Use this information to estimate the weights of other animals.

> This question develops students' ability to reason proportionally. For example, a fully grown Saint Bernard is about ten times the size of a medium-size cat, so it probably weighs about 60 kilograms. A cow is about one hundred times the size of a medium-size cat, so it could weigh 600 kilograms. This question can be reused with another benchmark weight and unit (e.g., pounds or grams).

6. White's Bakery uses 30-pound bags of flour. Its triple-layer cake uses 4 cups of flour. How many cups of flour do you think are in one bag of flour?

> In order to answer this question, students will need to estimate or find the weight of smaller amounts of flour. To help them with this, you may wish to provide

materials such as measuring cups, flour, and a spring scale. As a follow-up question, ask, "How many triple-layer cakes could be baked from one bag of flour?"

7. I bought medium-size packing boxes that each hold 20 kilograms to move to a new house. What objects might I put in one of these boxes?

> Since this question requires students to think about the weights of household objects, they may need to explore this question for homework. In addition, you may wish to provide them with the equivalence between pounds and kilograms to help them estimate the weights of various objects in kilograms.

8. Unpopped popcorn kernels are on one side of a balance scale and popped popcorn is on the other. How many of each might be on each side if the scale is level?

> This question requires students to consider the relationship between the weight of unpopped corn and the weight of popped corn. Students should find the weight of a group of kernels and a group of popped corn rather than the weight of each piece (since one kernel and one piece of popcorn is each so light).

9. Sheila emptied her piggy bank, wrapped her coins, and put them in a bag to bring to the bank. The bag weighed 20 pounds. How much money do you think Sheila had in coins?

> In order to answer this question, students will need to estimate or determine the weight of a roll of pennies, a roll of nickels, a roll of dimes, and/or a roll of quarters. You may provide students with these items or have them find the information for themselves.

Area (Grades 7-8)

EXPERIENCES AT THIS LEVEL WILL HELP CHILDREN TO

- estimate and measure the area of two-dimensional shapes and the surface area of three-dimensional shapes
- select appropriate units from both systems of measurement
- relate area to other attributes of a shape, such as side length
- use known areas to estimate unknown areas

MATERIALS

- 11-by-17-inch pieces of paper
- geoboards
- graph paper (see Blackline Masters)

Good Questions for Math Teaching

Good Questions and Teacher Notes

1. A banquet hall can seat 150 to 200 people. How big might this banquet hall be?

> One way to get started answering this question is to figure out how many people will sit at each table, how big that table will be, and how much space will separate each table. Then, apply proportional reasoning to estimate the size of the room.

2. I wrapped a rectangular box in a piece of wrapping paper that was 11 inches by 17 inches. I had no paper left over but did have some minor overlaps. What might have been the dimensions of my box?

> Have 11-by-17-inch paper available to help students answer this question.
>
> EXTENSION   This question can be extended by giving the size of a present to be wrapped and then asking students what size sheet of wrapping paper would cover it.

3. Find the length, width, and height of a rectangular prism that has a surface area of more than 200 square inches but less than 300 square inches.

> It will be interesting for students to discuss how they answered this question. Some students may choose to draw labeled sketches of the prism while others may choose to work directly with a formula for surface area.

4. Sketch a triangle with an area of 12.5 square inches. Label its base and height.

> To answer this question, students will need to apply their knowledge of rational numbers. Including rational numbers in the study of measurement is a great way for students to practice computation in a meaningful way. Have geoboards available on students' desks so that they can answer this question concretely as well as abstractly.

5. A ball of dough is rolled out into a circle with a 12-inch diameter. How many cookies with a diameter of 2.5 inches can be made from this dough?

> Some students may wish to answer this question by applying the area formula for circles—figuring out the area of the ball of dough, figuring out the area of each cookie, and dividing (assuming that all the dough is used up). Some other students may choose a visual approach wherein they draw a scaled picture of the dough and divide it into cookies that are also drawn to scale.

Measurement

6. A rectangle is approximately equal in area to a circle whose area is 49π square inches. What might be the length and width of this rectangle?

Watch for students who equate 49π square inches with 49 square inches.

7. Circle A has an area of 9π square units. Circle B has an area of 16π square units. Find the side length of a square whose area is greater than that of Circle A but less than that of Circle B.

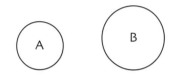

Students sometimes have difficulty interpreting measurements such as 9π and 16π. You may wish to discuss what these measurements mean before posing this question. One way to answer this question is to think of a square that is *circumscribed* around Circle A. Since Circle A must have a radius of 3, the square would have a side length of 6 and an area of 36, which is more than 9π but less than 16π.

8. I drew an irregular eight-sided figure. Only four sides were marked but that was still enough information to figure out the area of the entire figure. What might this figure have looked like?

Note whether students use symmetry and/or right angles to create their figures. As a follow-up question, ask students to find the perimeters of their figures.

9. A roll of wallpaper is 1 meter by 10 meters. How many rolls do you think would be needed to cover the walls of this classroom?

Decide whether students will measure or estimate the area of the walls of the classroom.

10. Create a square on a geoboard whose area is *not* a square number. How long is each side of your square?

The side length of the square will be the square root of the square units inside the square.

Length and Perimeter (Grades 7-8)

EXPERIENCES AT THIS LEVEL WILL HELP CHILDREN TO
- measure and estimate lengths and perimeters and circumferences
- use the Pythagorean theorem to find linear measurements

- estimate unknown lengths using known lengths
- reason proportionally to solve problems about linear measurement

MATERIALS

- geoboards or geoboard dot paper (fractions dot paper can be used; see Blackline Masters)
- rulers, meter sticks, and yardsticks

Good Questions and Teacher Notes

1. Juana is 5.6 feet tall and Jeremy is 5.8 feet tall. Liza is taller than Juana but shorter than Jeremy. How tall might she be in feet and inches?

This question is designed to address the misconception that 5.6 feet means 5 feet and 6 inches. If students believe this misconception, they will answer that Liza might be 5 feet and 7 inches, which is not correct. To help students see the flaw in this misconception, ask, "Is someone who is five and a half feet tall also five and six-tenths inches tall?" Since students are familiar with the decimal equivalent for half, they should see that since 6 inches is half of 12 inches, 5.5 feet would be equal to 5 feet and 6 inches.

2. A circle has a circumference of 36π centimeters. What might be the length and width of a rectangle that has a perimeter approximately equal to this circumference?

Watch for students who equate 36π centimeters with 36 centimeters.

3. One-centimeter-wide ribbon is wrapped around a spool that has a radius of 4 centimeters and a height of 12 centimeters. There are approximately three layers of ribbon wrapped around the spool. What might be the length in meters of the entire piece of ribbon?

This is a complex question that requires integrated knowledge of circumference, spatial visualization, linear measurement, and estimation.

4. A television screen measures 41" along its diagonal. What might be the length and width of the screen?

Finding the length and width of an object using the measure of its diagonal is a real-life application of the Pythagorean theorem. As a follow-up to this question, have students find print advertisements of other items measured by their diagonals (e.g., a computer screen) and use them to find their lengths and widths.

5. A 15-foot-tall ladder has a warning that reads "Bottom of ladder should rest between 3 and 4 feet from the wall." What are some heights that a person standing on the ladder can reach?

> Drawing a picture of the ladder leaning against a wall might help students see this question as an application of the Pythagorean theorem.

6. Create a right triangle on a geoboard whose perimeter is more than 5 but less than 10 inches.

> EXTENSION   Ask students to find the perimeters of nonright triangles.

7. The tip of an average person's thumb is about 1 inch in length. Use this information to think of objects that are approximately 1 foot and 1 yard long.

> Be sure to have students check at least some of their answers. This will develop their estimation skills since they will learn whether they tend to underestimate or overestimate and, more importantly, how to compensate for that.

8. If we wanted to draw a floor map of this classroom on an 8.5-by-11-inch piece of paper, what might be our scale?

> EXTENSION   Ask students to think of a scale that would allow them to draw the floor map of the school on an 8.5-by-11-inch piece of paper.

9. If all of the students in this school arrived at once and entered the building in a single-file line, how long do you think this line would be?

> One way to answer this question is to estimate the length of a single-file line for the students in one class and use proportional reasoning to estimate the length of a line for all the classes in the school.

10. Kara thinks that when both the length and the width of a rectangle are doubled, the perimeter is doubled. Than disagrees. He thinks that the perimeter will get four times bigger since that is what happens to the area. Whom do you agree with? Why?

> Pose this question after students have explored the relationship between scale factor and change in area. The fact that the perimeter doubles when the area quadruples is a common source of confusion for students. Spending time discussing why this makes sense will deepen students' understanding of perimeter as a linear measurement and area as a two-dimensional measurement.

Good Questions for Math Teaching

Volume and Capacity (Grades 7-8)

EXPERIENCES AT THIS LEVEL WILL HELP CHILDREN TO

- estimate and measure the volume of three-dimensional shapes and objects
- choose appropriate units to measure volume in both the customary and the metric system
- reason proportionally to solve problems about solid volume and liquid capacity

MATERIALS

- calibrated measuring cups or prisms
- common food items
- milk and juice cartons and/or three-dimensional models of prisms, pyramids, and polyhedrons

Good Questions and Teacher Notes

1. How are the methods of finding the volumes of polygonal prisms and cylinders similar and different?

> This type of compare-and-contrast question will help students connect what they are learning about volumes of different three-dimensional shapes rather than see each idea in isolation. For example, the formula "volume equals base times height" can be used for any polygonal prism and cylinder, *but* the methods for finding the area of the base vary according to the shape of the base.

2. A prism has approximately the same volume as a cylinder with a volume of 24π cubic inches. What might be the dimensions of this prism?

> Watch for students who equate 24π cubic inches with 24 cubic inches.

3. The surface area of a cylinder is between 200π and 300π square inches. What might be its volume?

> This is a complex question that takes many steps to answer. Reasoning through a question that incorporates both surface area and volume will strengthen students' understanding of each.

4. A cylinder holds exactly ninety-six cubes with a side length of 1 inch. What might be the dimensions of this cylinder?

Be sure to discuss at least one answer that approximates the value of pi and one that gives the answer in terms of pi.

5. Take four pieces of letter-size (8.5-by-11-inch) paper. Fold the papers into one tall and one short square prism and one tall and one short cylinder. Predict and then determine whether the volumes will be the same or different.
[Burns 2000]

> Many students predict that all four objects will have the same volume since all four pieces of paper are the same size. Volume, however, is not a function of surface area but rather the area of the base and the height of the container.

6. Could $1 million actually fit into a standard-size briefcase? Assume the largest denomination in circulation is $100.

> Since a black briefcase full of money is often a common feature on television and in the movies, students will enjoy the opportunity to verify or refute the claim of the $1 million contents.

7. The cylinder shown below holds three standard-size tennis balls. Give the dimensions for a rectangular box that will also hold three standard-size tennis balls.

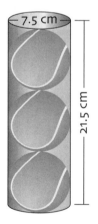

7.5 cm

21.5 cm

> Check to see whether students transfer the measurement of 7.5 cm to the box. Do they realize that both the length and the width must be at least 7.5 cm? As a follow-up question, ask, "Which has a greater volume: the cylinder or the rectangular box? Why?"

8. A piece of food displaces approximately 300 mL of water. What might the food be?

Have calibrated beakers or prisms and common food objects available for students to check and refine their answers.

9. You write on paper every day in school. If you were to box up all of the pieces of paper you've used since entering school, what fraction of this room do you think the boxes would fill?

To begin answering this question, students must estimate the size of the boxes they would use, how many papers would fit in one of these boxes, and how many papers they've written on in a typical year in school.

10. Our school cafeteria sells cartons of milk and cans of juice. Estimate how many milliliters of liquid are sold each week.

Adapt this question so that it reflects the type(s) and container(s) of liquids sold in your school's cafeteria. Have samples of these containers and/or calibrated measuring cups or prisms available to help students with their estimates. As a follow-up question, ask, "What size refrigerator is needed to hold a week's worth?"

11. One cubic centimeter of water weighs 1 gram. One thousand cubic centimeters equal 1 liter. Use this to estimate the weight of other objects when they are full of water: a fish bowl, a fish tank, a children's pool, a watering can, and so on.

Students will need to estimate the capacity of these objects and then use proportional reasoning to estimate their weights.

Blackline Masters

Graph Paper

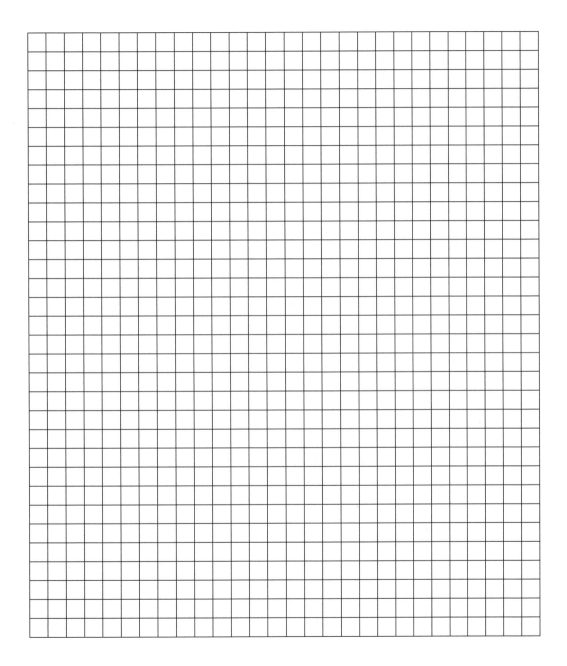

Fair Game 2

You need: a partner
                   a pair of dice

Rules

Take turns rolling the two dice. Player A scores a point if the sum is even. Player B scores a point if the sum is odd. Is the game fair? If not, how could you make the game fair? Explain your reasoning.

Play the game again, this time figuring out the product. Player A scores a point if the product is even. Player B scores a point if the product is odd. Is the game fair? If not, how could you make the game fair? Explain your reasoning.

From *Good Questions for Math Teaching, Grades 5–8* by Lainie Schuster and Nancy Canavan Anderson. © 2005 Math Solutions Publications

Dot Paper

From *Good Questions for Math Teaching, Grades 5–8* by Lainie Schuster and Nancy Canavan Anderson. © 2005 Math Solutions Publications

Pattern Block Figure

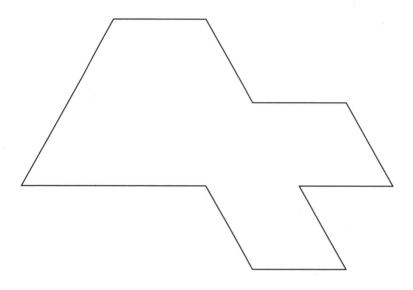

From *Good Questions for Math Teaching, Grades 5–8* by Lainie Schuster and Nancy Canavan Anderson. © 2005 Math Solutions Publications

Fractions Dot Paper

From *Good Questions for Math Teaching, Grades 5–8* by Lainie Schuster and Nancy Canavan Anderson. © 2005 Math Solutions Publications

6-by-6-inch Template

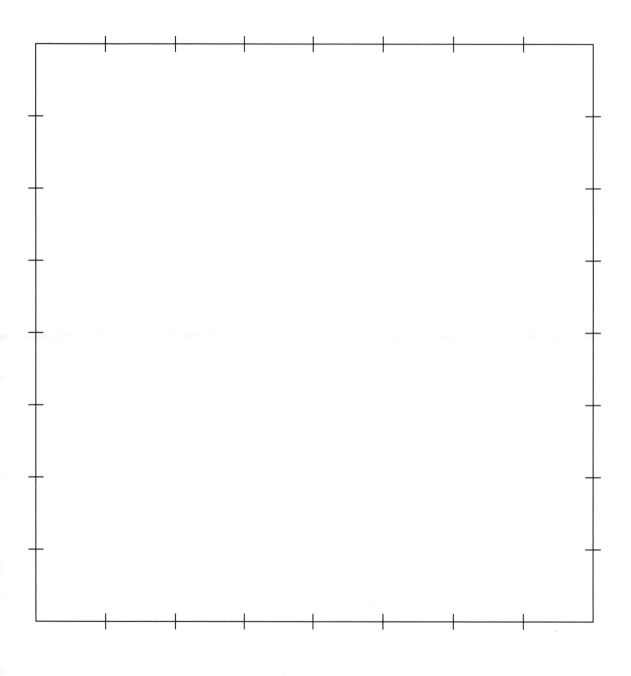

Hundredths Grid

From *Good Questions for Math Teaching, Grades 5–8* by Lainie Schuster and Nancy Canavan Anderson. © 2005 Math Solutions Publications

Tenths and Hundredths Grids

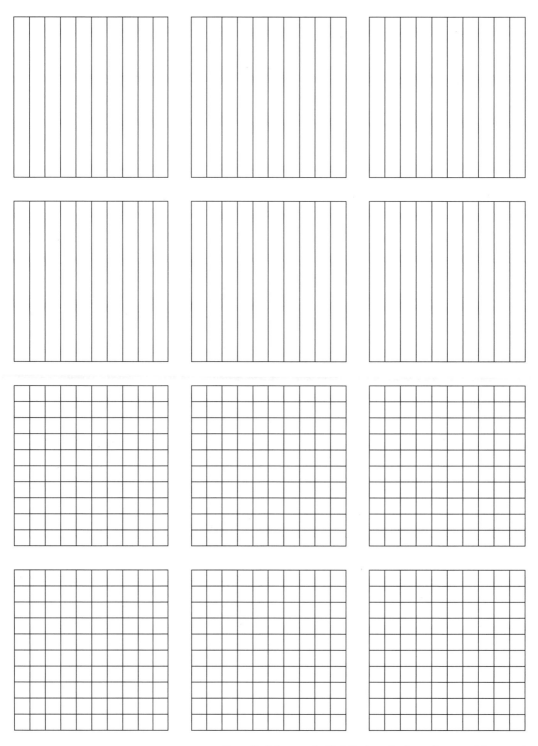

From *Good Questions for Math Teaching, Grades 5–8* by Lainie Schuster and Nancy Canavan Anderson. © 2005 Math Solutions Publications

∠HAT

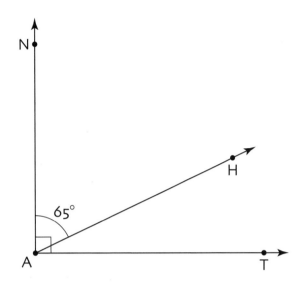

From *Good Questions for Math Teaching, Grades 5–8* by Lainie Schuster and
Nancy Canavan Anderson. © 2005 Math Solutions Publications

Clock Faces

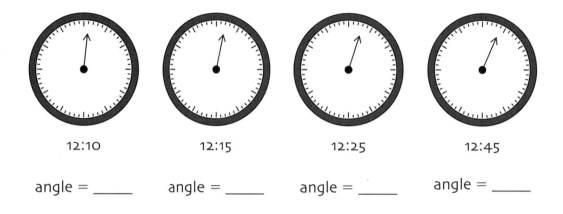

12:10

angle = _____

12:15

angle = _____

12:25

angle = _____

12:45

angle = _____

From *Good Questions for Math Teaching, Grades 5–8* by Lainie Schuster and
Nancy Canavan Anderson. © 2005 Math Solutions Publications

Polygon Sets

Set A

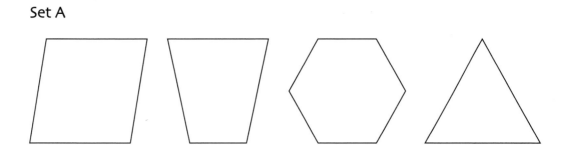

Set B

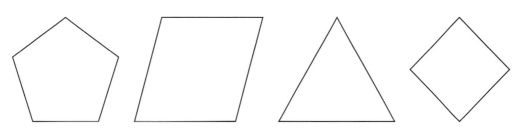

Set C

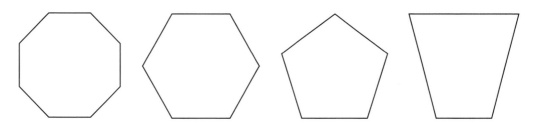

Rectangle ABCD

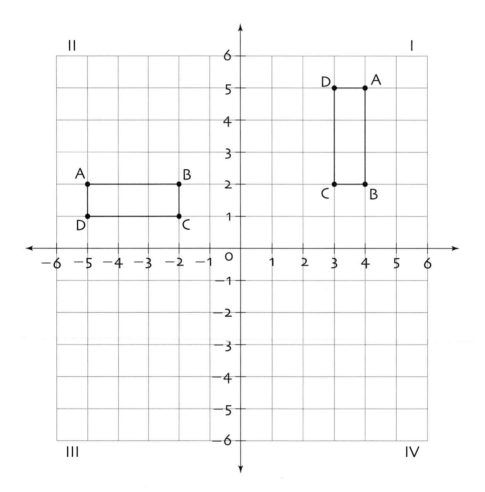

From *Good Questions for Math Teaching, Grades 5–8* by Lainie Schuster and
Nancy Canavan Anderson. © 2005 Math Solutions Publications

Flat Pattern Shapes

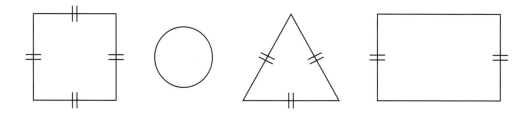

Number Path A

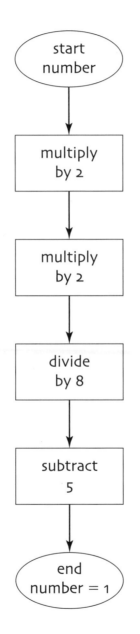

From *Good Questions for Math Teaching, Grades 5–8* by Lainie Schuster and
Nancy Canavan Anderson. © 2005 Math Solutions Publications

Number Path B

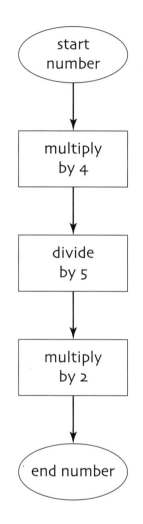

Patio Borders

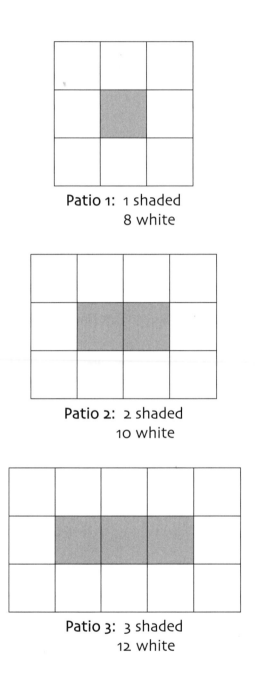

Patio 1: 1 shaded
8 white

Patio 2: 2 shaded
10 white

Patio 3: 3 shaded
12 white

From *Good Questions for Math Teaching, Grades 5–8* by Lainie Schuster and
Nancy Canavan Anderson. © 2005 Math Solutions Publications

Pencil Sharpener Stories and Graphs

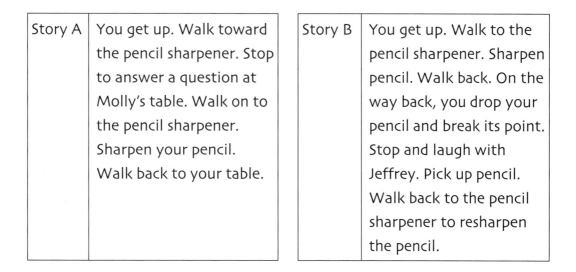

Story A	You get up. Walk toward the pencil sharpener. Stop to answer a question at Molly's table. Walk on to the pencil sharpener. Sharpen your pencil. Walk back to your table.

Story B	You get up. Walk to the pencil sharpener. Sharpen pencil. Walk back. On the way back, you drop your pencil and break its point. Stop and laugh with Jeffrey. Pick up pencil. Walk back to the pencil sharpener to resharpen the pencil.

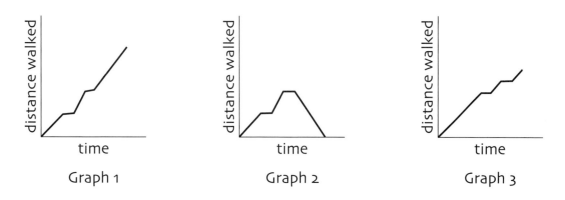

Graph 1

Graph 2

Graph 3

From *Good Questions for Math Teaching, Grades 5–8* by Lainie Schuster and
Nancy Canavan Anderson. © 2005 Math Solutions Publications

As Time Goes By Graphs

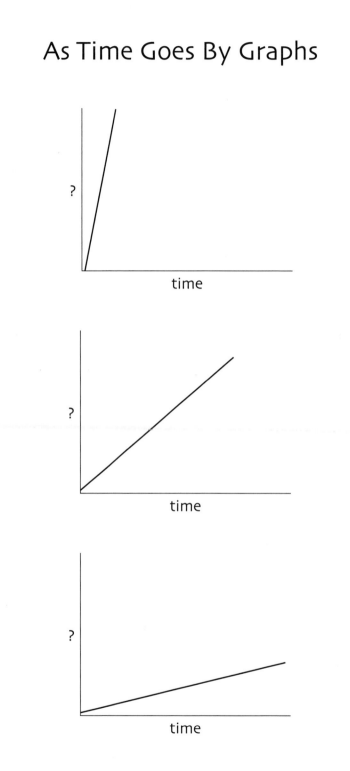

From *Good Questions for Math Teaching, Grades 5–8* by Lainie Schuster and
Nancy Canavan Anderson. © 2005 Math Solutions Publications

Grouping Patterns

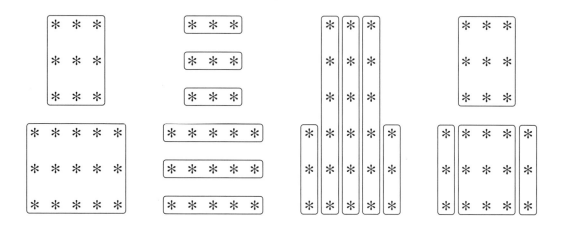

From *Good Questions for Math Teaching, Grades 5–8* by Lainie Schuster and
Nancy Canavan Anderson. © 2005 Math Solutions Publications

Toothpick Shapes and Tables

Side Length	Number of Toothpicks
1	4
2	8
3	12
10	40
n	$4 \times n$

Side Length	Number of Toothpicks
1	1
2	6
3	9
10	30
n	$3 \times n$

From *Good Questions for Math Teaching, Grades 5–8* by Lainie Schuster and Nancy Canavan Anderson. © 2005 Math Solutions Publications

Walk-a-Thon Graphs

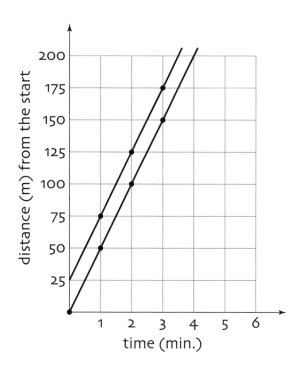

From *Good Questions for Math Teaching, Grades 5–8* by Lainie Schuster and
Nancy Canavan Anderson. © 2005 Math Solutions Publications

Candy Scatter Plot

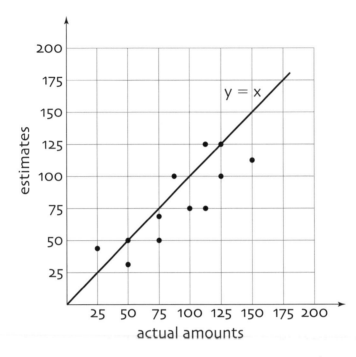

Perimeter and Area Tables

Side Length	Perimeter
1	4
2	8
3	12
10	40
n	$4n$

Side Length	Perimeter
1	1
2	4
3	9
10	100
n	$n \times n$

From *Good Questions for Math Teaching, Grades 5–8* by Lainie Schuster and Nancy Canavan Anderson. © 2005 Math Solutions Publications

Sunflower Growth

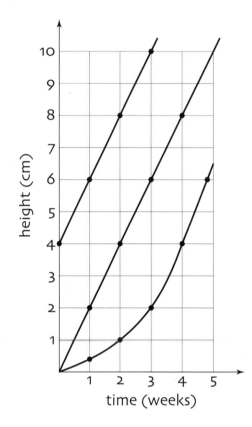

From *Good Questions for Math Teaching, Grades 5–8* by Lainie Schuster and
Nancy Canavan Anderson. © 2005 Math Solutions Publications

Mystery Line Plots

```
                        X
                  X  X  X
                  X  X  X  X     X     X
      X           X  X  X  X  X  X  X     X     X  X
52 53 54 55 56 57 58 59 60 61 62 63 64 65 66 67 68 69 70 71
```
Plot 1

```
                                 X
               X     X  X        X     X
X        X     X     X  X        X     X     X  X  X
48 50 52 54 56 58 60 62 64 66 68 70 72 74 76 78 80 82
```
Plot 2

```
    X
X   X
X   X   X
X   X   X
X   X   X   X   X   X   X
0   1   2   3   4   5   6
```
Plot 3

```
                     X
                  X  X     X     X
      X     X     X  X  X  X     X  X     X
26 28 30 32 34 36 38 40 42 44 46 48 50 52 54
```
Plot 4

```
                    X
        X           X       X   X
X       X   X       X   X   X   X       X
0   1   2   3   4   5   6   7   8   9   10
```
Plot 5

From *Good Questions for Math Teaching, Grades 5–8* by Lainie Schuster and Nancy Canavan Anderson. © 2005 Math Solutions Publications

Investment Graphs

Increase in Sales per Month

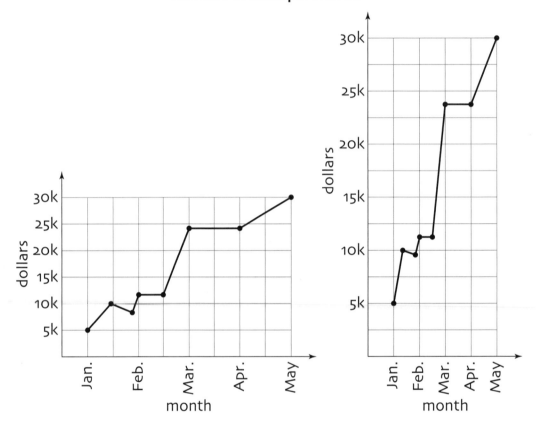

From *Good Questions for Math Teaching, Grades 5–8* by Lainie Schuster and
Nancy Canavan Anderson. © 2005 Math Solutions Publications

Dart Board

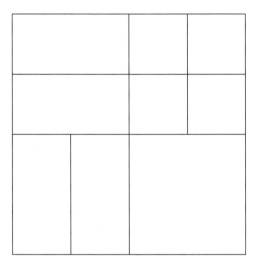

From *Good Questions for Math Teaching, Grades 5–8* by Lainie Schuster and
Nancy Canavan Anderson. © 2005 Math Solutions Publications

Bags of Marbles

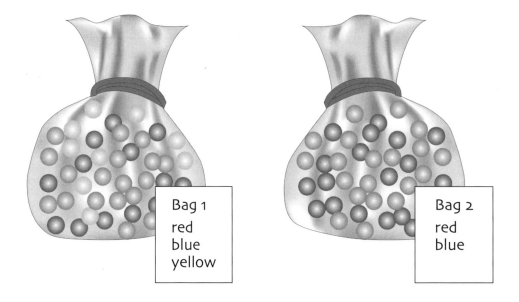

Bag 1
red
blue
yellow

Bag 2
red
blue

From *Good Questions for Math Teaching, Grades 5–8* by Lainie Schuster and
Nancy Canavan Anderson. © 2005 Math Solutions Publications

Blank Spinner Faces

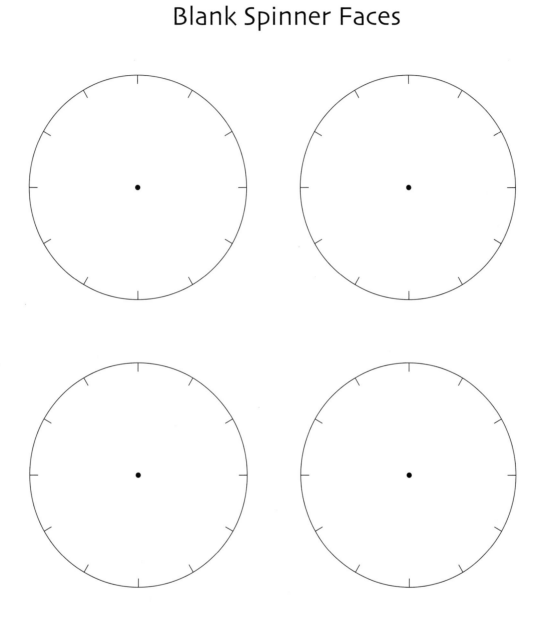

From *Good Questions for Math Teaching, Grades 5–8* by Lainie Schuster and Nancy Canavan Anderson. © 2005 Math Solutions Publications

Weights

From *Good Questions for Math Teaching, Grades 5–8* by Lainie Schuster and Nancy Canavan Anderson. © 2005 Math Solutions Publications

Irregular Polygon

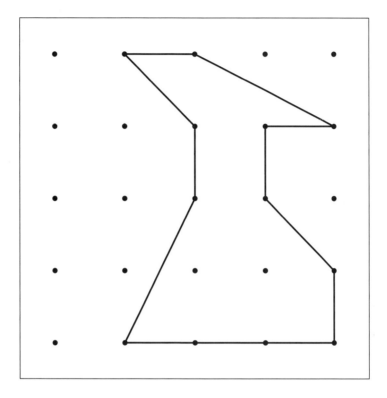

From *Good Questions for Math Teaching, Grades 5–8* by Lainie Schuster and
Nancy Canavan Anderson. © 2005 Math Solutions Publications

Cutout Polygon Models

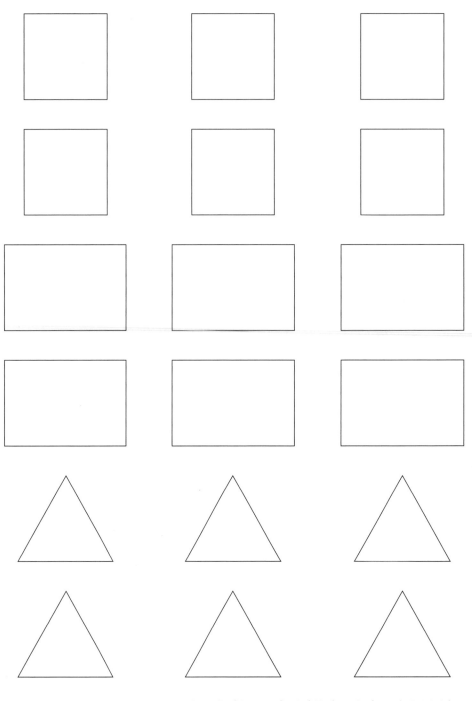

From *Good Questions for Math Teaching, Grades 5–8* by Lainie Schuster and Nancy Canavan Anderson. © 2005 Math Solutions Publications

Volume Pattern

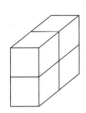

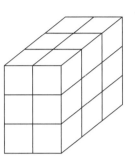

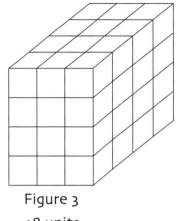

Figure 1   Figure 2   Figure 3

4 units   18 units   48 units

1 × 2 × 2   2 × 3 × 3   3 × 4 × 4

Prisms

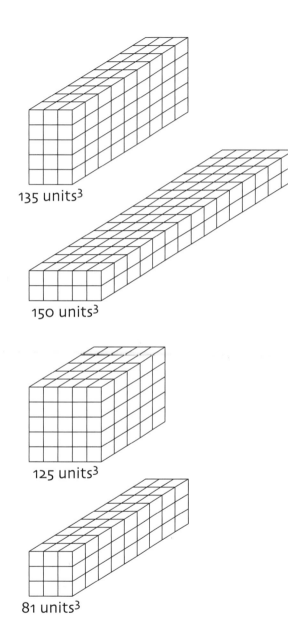

135 units³

150 units³

125 units³

81 units³

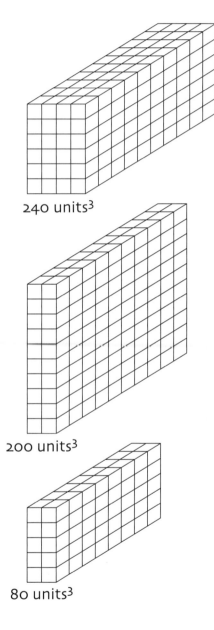

240 units³

200 units³

80 units³

From *Good Questions for Math Teaching, Grades 5–8* by Lainie Schuster and
Nancy Canavan Anderson. © 2005 Math Solutions Publications

References

Battista, Michael T., and Mary Berle-Carman. 1997. *Containers and Cubes: 3-D Geometry.* Investigations in Number, Data, and Space series. Glenview, IL: Scott Foresman.

Becker, Jerry P., and Shigeru Shimada. 1997. *The Open-Ended Approach: A New Proposal for Teaching Mathematics.* Reston, VA: National Council of Teachers of Mathematics.

Burns, Marilyn. 1992. *The Way to Math Solutions.* Sausalito, CA: Math Solutions Publications.

———. 2000. *About Teaching Mathematics: A K–8 Resource.* 2d ed. Sausalito, CA: Math Solutions Publications.

———. 2003. The Fraction Kit. Sausalito, CA: Math Solutions Publications.

Chapin, Suzanne H. 1997. *Middle Grades Math.* Upper Saddle River, NJ: Prentice Hall.

Chapin, Suzanne H., and Art Johnson. 2000. *Math Matters: Understanding the Math You Teach, Grades K–6.* Sausalito, CA: Math Solutions Publications.

Chapin, Suzanne H., Catherine O'Connor, and Nancy Canavan Anderson. 2003. *Classroom Discussions: Using Math Talk to Help Students Learn, Grades 1–6.* Sausalito, CA: Math Solutions Publications.

Collins, John. 1992. *Developing Writing and Thinking Skills Across the Curriculum: A Practical Program for Schools.* West Newbury, MA: Collins Education.

Costa, Arthur L., and Bena Kallick, eds. 2000. *Activating and Engaging Habits of Mind.* Alexandria, VA: Association for Supervision and Curriculum Development.

Cuevas, Gilbert J., and Karol Yeatts. 2001. *Navigating Through Algebra in Grades 3–5.* Reston, VA: National Council of Teachers of Mathematics.

Dantonio, Marylou, and Paul C. Beisenherz. 2001. *Learning to Question, Questioning to Learn: Developing Effective Teacher Questioning Practices.* Needham Heights, MA: Allyn and Bacon.

Everyday Learning Corporation. 2002. *Everyday Mathematics: The University of Chicago School Mathematics Project.* Chicago: Everyday Learning.

Greenes, Carole, and Carol Findell. 1998. *Groundworks: Algebra Puzzles and Problems.* Chicago, IL: Creative Publications.

Greenes, Carole, Linda Schulman Dacey, and Rika Spungin. 2001a. *Hot Math Topics, Grade 4: Estimation and Logical Reasoning.* Parsippany, NJ: Dale Seymour.

———. 2001b. *Hot Math Topics, Grade 4: Measurement and Geometry.* Parsippany, NJ: Dale Seymour.

———. 2001c. *Hot Math Topics, Grade 5: Algebraic Reasoning.* Parsippany, NJ: Dale Seymour.

———. 2001d. *Hot Math Topics, Grade 5: Fractions and Decimals.* Parsippany, NJ: Dale Seymour.

———. 2001e. *Hot Math Topics, Grade 5: Geometry and Measurement.* Parsippany, NJ: Dale Seymour.

Greenes, Carole, Linda Schulman, and Rika Spungin. 1989. *Thinker Math: Developing Number Sense and Arithmetic Skills, Grades 5–6.* Chicago, IL: Creative Publications.

Jacobs, Harold R. 1970. *Mathematics: A Human Endeavor.* New York: W. H. Freeman.

Juster, Norton. 1961. *The Phantom Tollbooth.* New York: Random House.

Lappan, Glenda, James Fey, William Fitzgerald, Susan Friel, and Elizabeth Phillips. 2002a. *Connected Mathematics Project: Bits and Pieces I.* Glenview, IL: Prentice Hall.

———. 2002b. *Connected Mathematics Project: Bits and Pieces II.* Glenview, IL: Prentice Hall.

———. 2002c. *Connected Mathematics Project: Comparing and Scaling.* Glenview, IL: Prentice Hall.

———. 2002d. *Connected Mathematics Project: Covering and Surrounding.* Glenview, IL: Prentice Hall.

———. 2002e. *Connected Mathematics Project: Filling and Wrapping.* Glenview, IL: Prentice Hall.

———. 2002f. *Connected Mathematics Project: How Likely Is It?* Glenview, IL: Prentice Hall.

———. 2002g. *Connected Mathematics Project: Moving Straight Ahead.* Glenview, IL: Prentice Hall.

———. 2002h. *Connected Mathematics Project: Prime Time.* Glenview, IL: Prentice Hall.

———. 2002i. *Connected Mathematics Project: Shapes and Designs.* Glenview, IL: Prentice Hall.

———. 2002j. *Connected Mathematics Project: Stretching and Shrinking.* Glenview, IL: Prentice Hall.

————. 2002k. *Connected Mathematics Project: What Do You Expect?* Glenview, IL: Prentice Hall.

Lawrence, Ann, and Charlie Hennessy. 2002. *Lessons for Algebraic Thinking, Grades 6–8.* Sausalito, CA: Math Solutions Publications.

McKenzie, Jamie. 2003. "Telling Questions and the Search for Insight." Accessed 20 December at www.questioning.org/Q8/telling.html.

Merrill, Jean. 1999. *The Toothpaste Millionaire.* Boston: Houghton Mifflin.

Meyer, Margaret, and Georgianna Diopoulos. 2002. "Special Needs Learning Anchored in Context." *Mathematics Teaching in the Middle School* 8: 16–21.

Miller, Elizabeth D. 2001. *Read It! Draw It! Solve It! Problem Solving for Intermediate Grades.* Parsippany, NJ: Dale Seymour.

Murray, Miki. 2004. *Teaching Mathematics Vocabulary in Context.* Portsmouth, NH: Heinemann.

Musser, Gary, and William Burger. 1988. *Mathematics for Elementary Teachers.* New York: Macmillan.

National Council of Teachers of Mathematics (NCTM). 2000. *Principles and Standards for School Mathematics.* Reston, VA: National Council of Teachers of Mathematics.

Sullivan, Peter, and Pat Lilburn. 2002. *Good Questions for Math Teaching: Why Ask Them and What to Ask, K–6.* Sausalito, CA: Math Solutions Publications.

Tierney, Cornelia, Beverly Cory, and Catherine Anderson. 1998. *Patterns of Change: Tables and Graphs.* Investigations in Number, Data, and Space series. Glenview, IL: Scott Foresman.

Van de Walle, John. 1998. *Elementary and Middle School Mathematics.* New York: Longman.

Wickett, Maryann, Katharine Kharas, and Marilyn Burns. 2002. *Lessons for Algebraic Thinking, Grades 3–5.* Sausalito, CA: Math Solutions Publications.